RABBI
SCHOLAR
FATHER
FRIEND

The Life, Thought,
Humor, and Wisdom of
Rabbi Edward M. Gershfield

JAMES N. GERSHFIELD

Scribal
Scion
Publishing

Rabbi Scholar Father Friend
The Life, Thought, Humor, and Wisdom of Rabbi Edward M. Gershfield

James N. Gershfield

Copyright (c) 2024 by James N. Gershfield, All Rights Reserved. No part of this book may be copied or reproduced in any way without explicit written permission from the publisher.

Cover design by James N. Gershfield

Disclaimer: The author and publisher specifically disclaim all responsibility for any liability, loss or risk, personal or otherwise, that is incurred as a consequence, directly or indirectly, of the use and application of any of the contents of this book.

ISBN-13: 979-8886650181, Paperback
ISBN-13: 979-8886650198, Hardcover

This book is lovingly dedicated to my late father Rabbi Edward M. Gershfield, of blessed memory

Published by Scribal Scion Publishing, Teaneck NJ, USA
Library of Congress Control Number: 2024943770

First Edition, published in 2024
Scribal Scion Publishing is an imprint of
Scribal Scion Publishing LLC
Please visit our website to learn more about us and our books:
https://scribalscionpublishing.com

Cover photos and all interior illustrations licensed from Adobe Stock

Other books by James N. Gershfield:
The Illuminated Omer Counting Book
The Illuminated Omer Counting Book Sephardic Edition
Rainy River Girl: A Memoir (co-authored with Toby M. Gershfield)

Contents

Why Read This Book	2
Introduction	3
Chapter 1 • Early Years in Canada	7
Chapter 2 • Becoming a Rabbi	23
Chapter 3 • A New Life at JTS in New York	27
Chapter 4 • Jewish and Roman Law	37
Chapter 5 • Jewish Divorce	45
Chapter 6 • Life as a Scholar	55
Chapter 7 • Father and Friend	71
Chapter 8 • Adult Education Courses	75
Chapter 9 • Sermons	87
Chapter 10 • Other Activities	99
Chapter 11 • Thoughts on Jews and Judaism	103
Chapter 12 • Words of Wisdom	137
Chapter 13 • Stories	145
Chapter 14 • Humor	151
Chapter 15 • Sayings and Expressions	163
Chapter 16 • Final Years, Months, and Days	173
Chapter 17 • List of Publications	177
About the Author	180

Rabbi Scholar Father Friend

Why Read This Book?

Every person is unique, which is a "truism", as my late father would say. However, some people have a very unusual combination of personal strengths, knowledge, insights and personality that make it worthwhile to get to know them and their life stories. This book is a biography of my father, the late Rabbi Edward M. Gershfield, of blessed memory. He passed away in 2019 at the age of 86, and combined a variety of qualities that made his life, thought, humor, and wisdom worth studying.

As the title of this book indicates, Rabbi Gershfield was a rabbi, a scholar, a father, and a friend. However, he also was a beloved teacher, an innovative thinker, a gifted orator, a respected adviser to other rabbis, an expert on comparative Jewish and Roman law, a beautiful singer of Jewish prayers, and a talented Hebrew scribe who administered and wrote many Jewish divorce documents, known as Gittin.

By reading this book, you will be introduced to his humble beginnings in the city of Winnipeg Manitoba, which he used to call "a very large, small town", his rabbinical training and ordination as a rabbi at the Jewish Theological Seminary of America in New York City, his doctoral studies at the University of Oxford in England, his life of teaching others about the Jewish religion, including some of his own thoughts about Judaism, his sense of humor, and his life as a Jewish divorce expert.

Introduction

In the Mishnah, the great work of Jewish oral law, in Tractate Bava Metzia, Chapter 2, Mishnah 11, it says: "Your father is the one who brings you into this world, but your rabbi is the one who teaches you wisdom and helps you get into the World to Come". In my case, both were true: My father was my rabbi, and my rabbi was my father. As the title of this book indicates, my father was also a scholar and a friend.

For several years toward the end of my father's life, I wanted to write a book together with him about some Jewish topic. However, the opportunity didn't present itself while he was still alive, and that goal of mine remained unfulfilled. Now that I have been granted the time and opportunity to write a book about his life and work, I feel in a certain way that he is writing this book with me, since I have been able to read and study many of his teachings in preparation for writing his biography and incorporating them into this book. In one sense, I couldn't have written this book without him. If you are ever given the opportunity to write a book together with either of your parents, my suggestion is that you make the most of the opportunity and don't pass it by, because it is such a special thing to be able to do while one's parents are still alive.

Rabbi Scholar Father Friend

One thing that my father used to do was to repeat the same stories and jokes over and over, and sometimes it became a little annoying having to listen to them repeatedly while I was growing up. However, as I grew older, and especially after my father passed away, I realized that he was using the same technique of teaching the Jewish laws and traditions that has been used for thousands of years by Jewish scholars and teachers. In the Book of Joshua 1:8 it says, "Don't allow the Torah to leave your lips, but rather repeat it day and night so that you will be able to observe everything that is written in it." This is the approach that my father took, possibly without realizing it consciously, to tell me things that he thought were important for me to learn and remember. I believe that it is specifically because of his repetition of many stories and words of wisdom that I have been able to remember so many of them.

This book was written from my perspective as his son, and is based on both my personal experiences and the knowledge that I have gained about his life from people who knew him, and from his writings and audio recordings.

Even though my father was ordained as a rabbi by the Jewish Theological Seminary of America in New York City (hereafter referred to simply as JTS), in his day-to-day career he was primarily a scholar and teacher, and he taught Talmud and Jewish Law at JTS from the time of his ordination until his retirement. One thing that made him stand out from his colleagues was that he didn't fit the standard cookie cutter mold of the typical rabbi or professor of Talmud. He was an independent thinker who was grounded in the traditional Jewish legal literature, and at the same time upheld traditional Jewish values, customs and beliefs. A "very rare bird" indeed, to use one of his own expressions.

Introduction

He used to include humor in his teaching, and he would typically begin each lecture with a humorous story or joke. This approach to lecturing is mentioned in the traditional Jewish literature as a proper thing to do, to make everyone feel more relaxed and open to learning. In Tractate Pesachim 117a, the Talmud says that the great Sage Rabba followed this practice. He would begin each lecture with humorous words, and then continue with a serious discussion of the law. In that spirit, if you start feeling that things are getting a bit too "heavy" when reading any part of this book, feel free to "lighten up" a bit and take a quick look at any of the jokes in Chapter 14 that my father used to tell, and then jump back to wherever you were in the book to continue reading.

Please remember, however, that even though humor is important, the study of Jewish laws and customs is not a joke. We need to take these things seriously, and to think about them critically and put effort into understanding them. At the same time, we need to have a certain amount of happiness and levity in our lives. As it is written in Psalm 100 verse 2 in Hebrew, "Ivdu et Hashem B'Simchah", which means "Serve God with happiness". Telling a little joke helps to soften the harshness of the legal discussions. It's like when you smear some cream cheese on a toasted bagel that has some sharp edges, and the cream cheese makes the bagel easier to chew, swallow, and digest.

When I decided to pursue a career in computer science, rather than study to become a rabbi like my late father, I didn't realize how much distance that decision would put between myself and him. As a teenager, I remember my father telling me that life as a rabbi, especially as a pulpit rabbi guiding the spiritual lives of a congregation, can be very difficult. All it takes, he would say, to turn the congregation against you is one person who doesn't like you for whatever reason, and that one person can cause all sorts of trouble. So much so, that the end result might involve having to leave that congregation and find another place to serve.

Working for a corporation as a software developer would be better, he used to say, because as long as you do a good job, it's much less likely that one person who doesn't like you will force you to leave your job. And if you really needed to go somewhere else, it wouldn't be too difficult to find employment at another company. However, the downside of that decision was that focusing on software technology made it difficult for me to relate to him sometimes, because he was very non-technical, and it wasn't easy discussing with him anything that I was learning in school or working on while on the job as a software engineer.

In many ways, my father was right. Working as a software engineer for over forty years allowed me to focus on my work, and not worry so much about whether someone liked me or didn't like me. It provided a relatively stable career. And over the years, I gradually came to understand that you don't need to be a pulpit rabbi to have a strong connection to Judaism and Jewish learning. As I got older, I gradually figured out a way to connect with my father in a way that we could both understand each other. That is the intended meaning behind the title of this book: "Rabbi Scholar Father Friend". My relationship with him developed over time from him being my rabbi, which never changed, to a scholar, to my father and finally to being my friend. Now that he is no longer with us in this world, this book is my tribute to his amazing and multi-faceted life.

Chapter 1

Early Years in Canada

First Days

My father used to like to tell the story of how he and his wife, my mother Toby Gershfield, were in the same room at the Winnipeg General Hospital when they were born in the Summer of 1933. My father was born only a few days before my mother, and he used to like to say that he looked around and noticed this nice Jewish baby girl in one of the baby bassinets, and he knew that he needed to keep a sharp lookout for her, and that one day they would be married, which they were. My mother told me that when she was a teenager and thinking about what sort of man she would want to eventually marry, she had a short list of must-have qualities in a man. She wanted to marry a Jewish man who observed Shabbat and the Kosher food laws, a non-smoker, non-alcoholic, and a non-drug addict. My father checked all of the boxes.

The Young Singer

My father had a beautiful voice as a child, and he maintained that nice voice throughout his life. It wasn't a very big voice, but it was pleasant to listen to. There was a Jewish children's choir in Winnipeg that was organized by Cantor Benjamin Brownstone, who was originally from Odessa, a city that spawned many great Cantors. My father was a member of that choir, and he used to refer to his last name as Broynshtayn, using a Yiddish accent. He also led services at the synagogue that he attended in Winnipeg.

In 1941, my father recorded a couple of Chanukah songs at a local radio station. He told me that at that time, it was difficult to find recording equipment that people could afford – this was before tape recording equipment was invented – and going to a radio station was one of the few ways that one could do it. The recording was made on a large 45 rpm record that only had one side (the other side was flat and had no grooves in it). His voice was beautiful and high pitched, since his voice had not yet gone through the change that male voices typically go through. He used to say that a boy's singing voice is very beautiful, although it only lasts for a short number of years, and if one can create a boys chorus in the synagogue, then it's a wonderful thing.

Prairie Expressions

Winnipeg is a city in the center of southern Canada, in a region known as the Canadian Prairies. The prairies are very flat. There are no mountains or even any small hills for miles and miles. My father used to say various things that he said were Prairie expressions. Here are some examples and their meanings:

"Dead as a doornail" – Completely dead.

"You can wait until the cows come home" – Apparently it can take a very long time for the cows to come back home after wandering away to find grazing areas.

"It doesn't amount to a hill of beans" – It doesn't amount to much at all. I've been told that in Regina, Saskatchewan people say, "It doesn't amount to a bag of beans".

"Totally bonkers" – Completely out of one's mind.

"Give a shiv in the ribs" – Similar to the American expression "stabbing you in the back".

"I'm impressed as all Hell" – I'm not really that impressed with what you just said.

"Deep, very deep" – Not really that deep.

"Dark as looking down a coal hole at midnight" – Very dark.

"Hootin' and hollerin'" - Making a lot of noise.

The Many Synagogues in Winnipeg

There were many synagogues in Winnipeg, because almost every family created its own synagogue. rabbis did not start their own synagogues – rather they would come to Winnipeg if they were invited by the local Jews who had the money to pay a rabbi.

My Zaida, which is a Yiddish word for grandfather, George Gershfield, was brought over by his older brother Yossi who was a junk dealer. That brother, Yossi, was the main person who started the Tiferes Yisroel shul in Winnipeg. George Gershfield had a special seat of honor on a raised platform in the front of the synagogue, and I remember seeing him sitting in that seat when I visited Winnipeg as a child.

How Cold Was It?

Winnipeg is known as the place in central Southern Canada where all of the cold air in the United States comes from. It is so cold in Winnipeg during the winter months that Psalm 147 verses 16 and 17 could be a good description of what it's like: "He puts down snow like wool, and spreads the frost like ashes. He throws down hail like little stones. Who can withstand the freezing cold?". Winnipeg has temperatures during the winter as low as 50 below zero Fahrenheit. And that's without any wind chill factor. The snow is like sand, so when the wind blows the snow hits you in the face and it can cause damage to your facial skin. In order to prevent injury, a good scarf has to be worn whenever walking outside. Also, the air is so cold in the winter that if you take a deep breath, you could freeze your lungs and end up in the hospital.

Amazingly, during the summer months, the temperatures get so high that all of the snow and ice melt and plants grow very well. This is only true in the Southern part of Canada where Winnipeg is situated. Areas further North don't warm up as much during the summer.

As an illustration of how cold it can get in the winters, my father used to tell this true story. One winter, the outside temperature was around negative 20 degrees Fahrenheit and there was a power outage. This meant that any heating system that relied on electricity stopped working and houses ended up freezing, unless they had a backup generator. There was one house that was owned by a butcher who had a special meat freezer in the basement which was designed to keep the meat at a constant temperature of 0 degrees Fahrenheit. A backup generator made sure that the freezer kept working even during a power outage. Since the temperature in the freezer was 20 degrees warmer than the outside temperature, the family went into the meat freezer to stay warm until the electricity was restored. Now that's cold!

Another story that my father used to tell about the cold weather in Winnipeg concerned a Native American man who was ill and was recovering in the Winnipeg General Hospital. He was used to living in extremely cold temperatures farther North in the remote parts of Manitoba. His hospital room was heated, and he just felt terrible due to the excessive heat in the room. The room had glass doors that opened onto a balcony. He asked whether the hospital staff could open those doors and push his bed onto the balcony so that he could get some fresh air. The staff did so, even though the temperature outside was below zero. Once the man's bed was on the balcony and he was exposed to the very low temperatures, he felt much better.

During the winters in Winnipeg, there was a lot of snow on the ground, and it was difficult to walk to synagogue for services on Shabbat. My father recalled what would happen when he would walk with his father to Shul on a Shabbat morning. His father would hold his hand, and if there was a pile of snow on the ground where my father needed to walk, his father would not stop walking. Instead, he would keep pulling on his hand so that my father would slide up and down on top of the snow pile next to his father, who was walking on the sidewalk. Once my father was past the snow pile, he could walk again on his own two feet on the sidewalk next to his father.

When people arrived at the synagogue on a Shabbat morning, after having suffered through an intense wintery blast during their walk to the synagogue, they would be served a little cake and whiskey to help them warm up before starting the service.

I remember visiting Winnipeg in the springtime, and seeing the gigantic chunks of ice flowing down the Red River as the temperatures started to rise and the ice started to break up.

The Talmud Torah in Winnipeg

Rabbi Abraham Kravetz was the principal of the Talmud Torah school. Mr. Klein was a Hebrew teacher, and he taught Mishnah to the boys once they got a little older. Also, Mr. Klein offered a Talmud class to those students who wanted to learn Talmud and were willing to come in to school on their own time. My father used to say that Mr. Klein gave him such a good grounding in the learning and understanding of Talmud that his Talmud studies in the Talmud Torah lasted him a lifetime.

When my father was a student at the Talmud Torah, the students would get together on Saturday afternoons to study Talmud. One Shabbat afternoon, my father came late to class. His teacher asked him why he was late. My father said that he was tired, so he took a nap, and that he was justified in doing so because the letters of the Hebrew word Shabbat (Shin, Beit, Taf) stand for the saying

"Sheina B'Shabbos Ta'anug", meaning "Sleep on the Shabbat is a pleasure". His teacher said that those letter could also stand for the words "Sheina B'Chol Ta'anug", meaning "Sleep on a regular weekday is a pleasure". So, my father replied, "Yes that true, and in fact that shows that taking a nap is always a good thing to do, whether it is on Shabbat or on any other day of the week."

Rabbi Kravetz had been a principal of a school in one of the large cities in Poland. He had spent some time in New York City, and therefore he was familiar with places like Rabbi Yitzchak Elchanan Yeshiva in Washington Heights, which is now part of Yeshiva University, and he advised my father not to go there since my father asked too many non-traditional questions, and he would probably not fit in very well in that environment.

Rabbi Kravetz had an idea of creating a new Jewish college within the University of Manitoba. That is why he wanted my father to get a Master's degree at Teachers College so that he could qualify to teach in the Talmud Torah high school (Rabbi Kravitz established a high school division within the Talmud Torah) and then eventually if he could get the rich Jewish men to donate money then he would create a "college" following all of the rules within the University of Manitoba, with their own building and many courses. This is probably because he had been a school administrator in Europe. Rabbi Kravitz was more of an educator (he was the rabbi at the Ashkenazi synagogue also).

One of the stories I remember my father telling about the Talmud Torah, or as he would affectionately call it "the Cheyder", was about one of the students who was not able to focus on his studies and was not doing well. The teacher was eventually able to determine that the thing that was bothering the student was that he really wanted a football so that he could play with it during his time off. Apparently, his family was too poor to afford to buy a football. So, the teacher took some of his own money and bought that student a football. The student was very happy, and was then able to focus on his studies and was very successful at school. The point of the story is that sometimes it is necessary to satisfy a desire of a student that might seem silly or not relevant to the studies, but which has the effect of impeding the student's success if the desire is not fulfilled.

Stories from His Youth

A person in Winnipeg had hired a man to mow their lawn. When the worker was done, and asked for payment, the person pretended to be praying Minchah (the afternoon prayer) and refused to be interrupted. The man who mowed the lawn waited a bit, and then tried to ask again for the two dollars that was owed him for the work. Again, the person pretended to be busy praying and too focused on prayer to be able to stop and pay the man. Finally, without saying a word, the person who was praying reached into their pocket and gave the man just one dollar. The man left in frustration and never got the second dollar that he was owed. My father would tell this story as an example of a Chillul Hashem (desecration of God's Name). Religion should never be used as a pretext for not paying workers the money that is due them. In fact, it is a sin according to the Jewish religion to not pay workers the full amount that is due them or to not pay them on time. The Torah contains a couple of verses that mention this requirement explicitly: Leviticus 19:13 and Deuteronomy 24:15.

When my father was very young, he took and passed the Jerusalem Examination which was, and still is, a standardized test of Hebrew for people who live outside the Land of Israel.

My father used to tell one of the stories that he heard from Rabbi Meir Schwartzman of Winnipeg. Rabbi Schwartman used to say that the Jews in Eastern Austria, an area known as Galicia, would say their prayers very quickly, the fastest in all of Europe. And the Jews in his home town prayed the fastest in all of Galicia. And the Jews in the synagogue where he prayed were the fastest of all of the synagogues in his town. Why did they rush through their prayers so quickly? He said that praying very quickly doesn't give the Satan a chance to do any harm. He would make the following analogy: If some people are riding in a sleigh pulled by horses, and a wolf is pursuing the sleigh, they will try to make the horses run faster and faster to outrun the wolf. The wolf is like the Satan chasing people who are saying their prayers.

Hebrew Name

My father's Hebrew name was Yitzchak Moshe ben Yuzpa, which means Yitzchak Moshe the son of Yuzpa. Isaac is the English form of the Hebrew name Yitzchak, which was the name of one of Abraham's sons as described in the book of Genesis, and Moses is the English form of the Hebrew name Moshe.

My father used to talk quite a bit about his father's name, "Yuzpa", and its derivation. Apparently, the name is a form of Yosef (usually translated as Joseph in English), but it is not exactly Yosef. The actual name is something like "Yoy-zip", with a hard "p" sound at the end. This hard "P" sound at the end of a name is not normal among Hebrew names. It is difficult to pronounce, and very few Hebrew words end with a hard "P" sound.

I found a number of articles that my father had saved about the name Yuzpa and about the famous Jewish people who had that name. He also had a Jewish book called "Get Mesudar", which discusses how to spell people's names in a Jewish divorce document, which is known as a Get in Hebrew. As an indication of how much he studied that name, my father wrote a note inside the front cover of his copy of Get Mesudar referring to the page number where the name Yuzpa is mentioned.

Whenever my father would sign a certificate of Jewish Divorce after a Get was delivered, he would write the letter "Peh", which has the sound of the letter P in English, in the middle of the name Yuzpa as a very large letter. It became a recognizable sign among those who knew my father as a Mesader Gittin, which is a Get administrator, and a Gittin Scribe, which is the person who actually writes the Get using a feather pen.

Bar Mitzvah

My father told me that when he became a Bar Mitzvah, after the Shabbat services in the synagogue they served a very simple Kiddush of just some cake and some drinks. His Bar Mitzvah occurred in 1946 not that long after World War Two ended, and people didn't have a lot of money to pay for a large Kiddush, even for as important an event as a Bar Mitzvah celebration.

The Machray School

The Machray School was a public elementary school in Winnipeg. It is interesting to note that my father did not attend a Yeshiva or a Jewish Day School. Rather, he attended a secular public school, with supplementary Jewish education at the Talmud Torah. The point is that it is possible to attain very high levels of scholarship in Jewish studies without having attended a Yeshiva or Day School as a child. What is important is that one have a strong dedication to study, and to not be distracted by all of the things that can interfere with study.

Saint John's High School

My father attended the Saint John's High School in Winnipeg. There, he learned how to make things from wood, including a beautiful tie rack for which he received a grade of 91/100. My mother also attended Saint John's High School.

Studying the Latin language was common in those days, and my father started studying Latin then. As it turns out, knowing Latin is a very useful skill for scholars, since many of the older books and writings on religion were written in Latin.

One thing that I didn't know about my father until I started doing the research for this book was that he played the starring role in a production of Gilbert and Sullivan's *Pirates of Penzance* in high school. That explains why he used to talk so much about Gilbert and Sullivan, and sing various songs from their plays.

An important lesson that we can learn from my father's experiences in his youth is that you don't have to go to a Yeshiva day school as a child in order to develop into a great Jewish scholar. However, it is good having Jewish education available at least as a part-time activity to help instill a love of learning Jewish texts and ideas. The schooling is just a beginning anyway, and it is up to each person to devote regular time in their adult lives to study and intellectual growth.

The House

My father's father was very handy, being a tinsmith by vocation, and made a number of improvements to the family home. One thing he did was to create a small compartment in the outer wall, with a little door on the outside and another door on the inside. When the milkman delivered the fresh milk in glass bottles, he could put the bottles in the small compartment and close the little door from the outside. This would help to prevent the milk from freezing in the winter.

Another thing that his father did was to install a screw-driven loader to automatically move coal from the coal bin in the basement into the boiler, which kept the house warm and provided the hot water. The screw was a long piece of metal shaped literally like a screw, and it was controlled by a thermostat. Whenever the temperature went below a certain preset level, a motor would turn on and rotate the screw, which would slowly move fresh coal into the furnace.

Zaida Gershfield

The Yiddish word that Ashkenazic Jews use when referring to their grandfather is Zaida. In some remote parts of New York City the word is pronounced Zaidy. When I was growing up, we always called my father's father, whose English name was George, Zaida Gershfield, to distinguish him from my mother's father, whom we also called Zaida.

Zaida Gershfield worked as a tinsmith at the Winnipeg General Hospital. Over the years, he developed a very strong grip in his hands from manually cutting sheets of metal using a hand cutter.

Even when he was in his 80's, he had a lot of power in his grip.

How NOT to Lose Weight

George Gershfield had become a little overweight, and his doctor told him that he needed to go on a diet. He told him to start using a "diet shake" that would provide all of the nutrition that he needed to lose weight. So, he started using the shake regularly and was excited to hear how much weight he had lost at his next doctor visit. After his doctor weighed him, he was surprised to discover that he had actually put on weight instead of losing it. The doctor asked him whether he had been using the diet shake. "Yes, of course" replied my grandfather. Then the doctor asked him how often he was taking it and how he prepared it. My grandfather explained that he was following the preparation directions very carefully, and he was having one of the shakes at every meal, in addition to his regular meals. The doctor then explained that the shake was supposed to be taken INSTEAD OF a meal, not IN ADDITION TO a meal.

A Kick in the Pants

At some point George Gershfield developed a cigarette smoking habit. He believed that it was not good for his health, but he was having trouble breaking the habit. So, he came up with an idea. He told his non-Jewish coworkers at the Winnipeg General Hospital where he worked that if any of them saw him smoking at the hospital, they had his permission to give him a swift kick in the pants. Needless to say, many of his coworkers would have been happy to oblige and would have kicked him very hard if given the chance. Apparently this strategy worked, and in a short time he had stopped smoking cigarettes.

Two Speeds

When George Gershfield was older, in his seventies and eighties, he used to like to say that he had two speeds when he would walk: slow and stop.

My Uncle Max

My father had a half-brother, Max, who was about 20 years older than him. My uncle Max was the only child of my grandfather's first wife. After his mother passed away at a relatively young age due to illness, my father's father remarried a woman named Leah. My father was the only child of that second marriage. My grandmother Leah also passed away at a relatively young age due to illness. When she was sick, her family called her Chaya Leah, because the name Chaya in Hebrew comes from the word that means "life", and it was believed that by calling her that, perhaps God's mercy would be increased, and He would help save her from her illness. For many years I thought that her name was Chaya Leah, because that's how my father always referred to her, but it was actually just Leah in Hebrew and Lily in English. My father lost his mother when he was only 17 years old. I never met her. However, I have seen photos of her.

When my uncle Max was young, my grandfather gave him some career advice. He told him that in order to avoid working in the sewers, like many uneducated people did, he should go to school and study something professional, like engineering. Max took his advice, studied electrical engineering, and earned a PE (Professional Engineer) license. Eventually, he landed a good job working for the Chicago Sanitary District. One of the main things that he did was designing industrial lighting for buildings. He also ended up designing the lighting for the sewers in Chicago. At that point, ironically, he was able to tell my grandfather that even with all of the advanced engineering education, he still ended up working in the sewer!

Deciding to Become a Rabbi

Something happened when my father was in Winnipeg that made him want to become a rabbi. What makes someone decide to become a rabbi? I suppose it depends on the person. I never thought to ask my father what made him want to become a rabbi, and that's one thing that I regret not doing. One guess is that his primary Jewish studies teacher in Winnipeg, Mr. Klein, gave him a thorough understanding of Judaism and Jewish law, and that probably gave him the desire to learn more and to teach others.

I don't think that my father really wanted to be a congregational rabbi. He exhibited strong ability in understanding legal concepts, and at one point early in his career I think he was considering becoming a full-time attorney as a way of earning a living. But that would have meant not being able to spend much time with his family, and raising a family was very important to both my father and my mother.

My mother helped to persuade my father that becoming a practicing lawyer would mean very long hours away from home, and would be detrimental to family life. As it turned out, my father used to emphasize the importance of the family and how each person plays their role in it. He practiced what he preached. Rabbi Kravetz steered my father toward applying to the Rabbinical School of JTS because he had an inquiring mind. Rabbi Kravetz thought that any of the major Orthodox Rabbinical Schools would be too limiting on his desire to do research and think about the development of Jewish Law, and comparing Jewish Law with other legal systems. As he found out after visiting a number of Yeshivot (the plural of the word Yeshiva), there tends to be a fixed set of questions that students learn, along with the acceptable answers to those questions. Students are encouraged to come up with original answers to the established set of questions. However, students who come up with new questions that aren't on the approved list will probably be seen as too radical, and won't fit in.

Chapter 2

Becoming a Rabbi

First Days in New York City

My father used to tell the story about the first few days in New York City after moving from Winnipeg to start his studies at the Rabbinical School of JTS. In Winnipeg, and in most other cities in the world, the daytime is the part of the day when activity occurs and there is noise outside, and the evenings are generally a quieter time when people are eating dinner or perhaps reading or watching television. But in New York City, my father noticed that the level of noise didn't change much at the end of each day. People were constantly walking around on the streets, sirens from police cars and ambulances could be heard, taxis made noise all night honking their horns, and the city buses made loud engine noises very late into the night. Eventually, he realized that New York City truly is "the city that never sleeps".

Rabbi Scholar Father Friend

Entrance Exams

Entrance exams for the JTS Rabbinical School took place during the summer. When my father travelled to JTS to take the entrance exams, he was wearing a heavy wool suit from Winnipeg. While everyone else was dying from the summer heat, amazingly my father stayed cool and calm. He was asked to read and explain some pages of the Talmud by Professor Boaz Cohen. My father did so without hesitation in Yiddish, since that is how he always learned Talmud growing up in Winnipeg. After he was done, Professor Cohen said, "That was great, but can you do it in English?" My father responded, "I don't know, I've never tried". But my father proceeded to do it in English very well. My father only spoke Yiddish at home, but spoke English at school. Therefore, he was fluent in Yiddish, and was fluent in English.

Apparently the plan was for my father to return to Winnipeg to head a new Jewish studies department within the University of Manitoba that Rabbi Kravetz was trying to establish. The funds were supposed to be raised from a wealthy benefactor in Winnipeg. Unfortunately, that person was not able to come up with the funds, so the new department did not materialize. As a result, my father stayed in New York and accepted a teaching position as a junior member of the faculty at JTS.

One of the things that all Rabbinical School students were expected to do was to give a Senior Sermon at the Shabbat morning services at JTS. My father used to tell the story about the senior rabbinical student who decided to play a little trick on Professor Alexander Marx. Professor Marx was prone to dozing off during the sermons. The student's senior sermon included the history of Alexander the Great, and how significant he was to world history. At one point in the sermon, the student said something like "Alexander marks the end of one era and the beginning of another. He said the words "Alexander marks" in a very loud voice, which caused Professor Marx to suddenly wake up and wonder why his name was being called.

Once, while a student, my father got sick and had a sore and swollen throat. He called a doctor, who came to the apartment to see what was wrong (doctors made house calls in those days). The doctor took a quick look, and then started asking my father lots of questions about his studies in the Rabbinical School, how life was in the Big Apple, and so on. Finally, the doctor was starting to leave the apartment and my father said, "Wait, what about this?", pointing to his throat. The doctor said, "Oh that's just a cold, don't worry about that. It will go away in a few days."

Crime and Books

When my father began his rabbinical studies at JTS he used to go frequently to the JTS library to read and study. There was an incident that occurred one evening during that time which caused my mother to get very nervous about my father walking on the streets of Manhattan at night in order to go to the JTS library. She wanted him to stop going so frequently, and especially at night.

In the 1950's, there was no Internet, no personal computers, no smartphones and no eBooks. So, the only way to read books was to either go to the library or buy the books that you needed and maintain a personal library at home. That was the time when my father started buying his own books so that he could study at home and not have to travel at night to the library.

Chapter 3

A New Life at JTS in New York

Shabbat at the Seminary

On Friday evenings, the Kabbalat Shabbat service was held in the synagogue which you would get to by turning left after entering the main entrance. I remember that there was a special holder on the wall that could hold a couple of plaques with words on them. They could be easily inserted and removed as needed during the year. In the Jewish prayers, there are a couple of phrases that are added only during certain times of the year, and the holder on the wall served as a handy reminder. I thought that was a great idea to help people remember which phrase to use in their prayers, and I have never seen that kind of sign anywhere else. Synagogues should consider installing a sign like that to remind their congregants which phrases to use throughout the year.

Rabbi Scholar Father Friend

I remember attending Shabbat services at the Seminary in the basement of the building to the right after entering the main entrance. A winding staircase led to a lower level that had a sort of waiting area with a table covered with people's Tallit bags, and beyond the table were the doors that led to the room that served as a sanctuary. I have fond memories of sitting next to my father during the morning Shabbat services on the chairs along the left wall of that room. Now and then, my father would point out something interesting in the Siddur (prayer book) or in the Torah reading. Those were some of the best experiences of my life.

There is a trend these days for children, once they get close to Bar Mitzvah age or even before, to stop sitting with their parents and instead to attend a special service limited to children. In my opinion, this is not a great idea. And it's sad, because it deprives children of that very special experience of sitting with their parents during the prayer services. This is something that can only be done for a limited number of years, and in a short time the opportunity is gone forever. Sitting with one's children during services creates memories that can last a lifetime.

One of my favorite things to do during the services was to wrap the Torah scroll, known in Hebrew as Gelilah, and to sit with it on the side of the stage while someone read the Haftarah. It is one of the great things to do, especially for young people, because it lets you hold the Torah close to you and it gives you a special feeling of closeness to the Torah. You literally wrap your arms around the Torah and give it a hug for several minutes. Over the years, I have noticed that there are some synagogues where the Torah scroll is placed in a special stand on the side of the Bimah, instead of someone sitting and holding it. I feel that this is not a good practice, since it eliminates the possibility for anyone, especially children, to get that feeling of close connection with the Torah scroll.

It should be noted that holding the Torah scroll during the Haftarah is an Ashkenazic custom. Some, but not all, Sephardic Jews have a custom of storing the Torah scroll in a specially constructed, and ornately decorated, container that can be opened and closed to facilitate reading from the scroll. But that Sephardic Torah scroll container, which is usually quite heavy since it also contains the Torah scroll inside of it, is not normally held by anyone during the Haftarah reading. Instead, it is placed on the lectern in a closed position and remains there during the reading of the Haftarah.

Another thing I remember occurred during the Shabbat morning services. There was separate seating of men and women, but no physical divider, known in Hebrew as a Mechitzah, between the two seating areas. There was just a wide aisle. This made it easier for male and female students who attended the service to stand in the back of the room and schmooze with each another during the service. My father didn't think that this was an appropriate thing for them to be doing, and it definitely bothered him.

Standing Around After Shabbat Services

We would stand together for at least 30 minutes or more after the Musaph service was over, while my father would talk with the other professors. I can't remember what any of the discussions were about, but I know that I was happy that my father was able to engage in discussions with other members of the faculty, and I felt very proud to be standing there with him.

Buying Books at JTS

I tended to spend a certain amount of time in my father's office, especially while I was attending courses at the undergraduate level at JTS, and I remember seeing a certain gentleman with a nice beard at the Seminary, and he would visit my father in his office regularly. He would bring a large bag filled with Jewish books, and my father would look at them carefully and would usually end up buying at least one or two books. I never knew whether my father really needed the books, or perhaps he was just trying to be helpful to the man with the books, but most likely the books that my father bought from that man were good scholarly books that were worth buying.

Bar Mitzvah Invitations

When my Bar Mitzvah was coming up, we needed to create invitations to send to invited guests. I remember being at the Seminary together with my father, and we were looking at the options for invitations that could be ordered. The person who was showing us the choices of paper and ink mentioned casually that, of course, my father would be doing the Hebrew lettering manually rather than using printed type, since it was well known around the Seminary that he was an excellent scribe.

At the time, I didn't think about the effect of saying "No thanks, I would rather have printed type", but that's what I said. The person was taken aback, and told me "But you know who your father is, right? Anyone else would be very honored to have him write the Hebrew part of their invitation by hand." I didn't realize that I was being disrespectful to my father, and I insisted on having printed type, arguing that the printed Hebrew characters are perfectly shaped, and hand-written characters could not be perfect. I must have valued perfection over human relations.

Even though I didn't want the Hebrew lettering to be done by hand, I created a monogram using ornate English letters for my initials on the front side of the invitations. I think it was my artistic side that made me want to do that.

Professor Saul Lieberman

Professor Saul Lieberman, of blessed memory, used to assign the Aliyot to the Torah on Shabbat mornings in the basement synagogue at JTS. Whenever a member of the graduating class of the Rabbinical School was scheduled to give his senior sermon at the services, the tradition was for that student to be assigned the fourth Aliyah, known as the Revi'i Aliyah. If there was no senior sermon that Shabbat, then Professor Lieberman used to assign the fourth Aliyah to himself. He wanted to make the point that all of the Aliyot are important, and people should not avoid being called up to the Torah reading for the Fourth Aliyah, which is considered by many Jews to be the least desirable Aliyah to the Torah.

My father used to quote Professor Lieberman as saying that "The clever man is able to get out of a bad situation that the wise man is able to avoid in the first place".

Early on in my father's career at JTS, Professor Lieberman told my father that he needed to decide: Is he a rabbi or a cantor? If he is going to be a rabbi, then he needs to stop leading the services like a cantor. Because of this, my father stopped leading the services at JTS, which is very unfortunate since he had a nice voice and did a great job leading the services.

Preparing Teaching Materials

My father used to prepare a lot of handouts for his students. One of the things that I noticed he would do was to number the lines of the Talmud text. He would make a copy of the pages that he wanted to teach and would write the line number on every fifth line. So, from the top of the page to the bottom of the page, the following line numbers would be used: 5, 10, 15, 20, etc. Then, he would make multiple copies of the page with the line numbers. This made it easier for him and his students to refer to specific lines within the text of the Talmud as he was teaching.

Too Many Meetings

One time my father wanted to avoid going to a scheduled meeting. As the date was approaching, a colleague at JTS asked my father whether he would be attending the meeting. My father said that he couldn't attend because he was scheduled to take a nap at that time. His colleague thought that my father was kidding, but he proceeded to show his colleague the entry in his date book for the date and time of the meeting and it clearly showed an entry that said, "Take nap".

An Early User of Technology

My father was ahead of his time in the use of technology to do his work as a scholar and teacher. As far as I know. he was the first professor at JTS to use a telephone answering machine. I remember, when I was a child, going into the JTS building on the left and seeing human telephone operators sitting in front of large telephone switchboards connecting incoming phone calls to their recipients, and connecting outgoing phone calls to the long-distance network. So, you can imagine how technologically advanced a telephone answering machine must have seemed at that time to the other members of the faculty.

Rabbi Philip Alstat

When I was in high school and college, I got to know Rabbi Philip Alstat, of blessed memory, who performed conversions of non-Jews to Judaism. I served as a witness for a few of the conversions, and weddings of converts that Rabbi Alstat had converted.

One day, after serving as a witness to a wedding, I came home, and my father asked me what the Hebrew names of the bride and groom were. I answered that I couldn't remember. When my father heard my response, he was not happy and said, "What's the point of being a witness if you can't remember the names of the people getting married? What if someone asks you later about the wedding, and you can only say 'I don't know'? If you are going to be a witness, you should be able to remember the names of the people getting married." That's when it became very clear to me that I had trouble remembering people's names, a challenge that I still have today.

Upon the occasion of my Bar Mitzvah, Rabbi Alstat wrote a very beautiful letter of congratulations to my parents.

Rabbi Alstat had a newspaper column that he wrote called "Strange to Relate", which is a translation of the Latin phrase "mirabile dictu".

Rabbi Alstat used to say that people can excel in four areas: Athletics, mathematics and logical thinking, money and business, and being handy with your hands. It is rare for a person to be really good in more than one of these areas. And it is extremely unusual for one person to excel in all four areas.

The Cafeteria

In addition to providing Kosher food for JTS faculty, staff, and students, the cafeteria at JTS was a place where students could spend some quality time speaking with my father as they ate lunch.

More Degrees

Soon after receiving his rabbinical ordination from JTS, my father enrolled in a Master's degree program in Latin at Columbia University. Latin is a very important language to know if you are a scholar, and especially if you want to be able to read many of the older commentaries written by non-Jews about Judaism or related subjects. Another important reason to be able to read and understand Latin fluently is in order to be able to read articles and books relating to Roman Law, and to read the various Roman legal codes in their original language. As you will see in the next chapter, my father embarked on a doctoral course of study in Oxford in order to become an expert on Roman and Jewish law.

In addition to working on a Master's degree in Latin, my father enrolled in a Master's degree program in Education at Columbia University's Teachers College (TC). I never understood why he did that until many years later, when I found out that the original plan was for him to go back to Winnipeg and become the leader of a new department of Jewish studies at the University of Manitoba.

Chapter 4

Jewish and Roman Law

After his rabbinical ordination, my father became increasingly interested in comparative law, and its importance in helping us to understand one's own legal system, whatever that is. In his case, he was especially interested in comparisons between Roman and Jewish law, and understanding what can be learned by comparing them.

When one reads the Talmud, one can take a simple approach of studying it as a standalone body of Jewish law, together with all of the traditional commentaries, such as Rashi, the Tosafot, Maharsha, and so on. The traditional commentaries seek to explain the basic meaning of the words of the Talmud, and to clarify various points of the law. Similarly, studying all of the Responsa that have been written over the last 1,000 years by various great rabbis and Jewish scholars can help clarify how to apply the law to certain cases and situations that have arisen.

However, taking that simple approach, which can occupy one's entire life because of the vastness of the legal material, omits an important aspect of Jewish law. And that aspect involves the fact that Jewish law is a particular legal system in a world of legal systems. Other legal systems exist and have existed in the world, and if we ignore all of those other legal systems when we study the Jewish legal system we will inevitably end up with a less accurate understanding of how the Jewish law truly developed and why certain things are the way that they are in Jewish law.

Laws in various countries can be split into two main types of law: Codes, where a written text sets out what the laws are and what the consequences are for not following them; and Common Law, where the laws are based on court cases and how judges have decided those cases. The Jewish law is mainly the first type, namely a Code. It is primarily a system of codes that together make up the body of Jewish law. The only other main body of law that has existed for over 2,000 years is the Roman Law, which is also a legal system. It follows logically that studying the Roman Law as a system of law can help give us insights into what a system of law involves. My father recognized this, although he wasn't the first scholar to realize this, and devoted a large amount of time and energy to the study of Roman law in order to better understand the workings of the Jewish law as a legal system.

Another influence on my father regarding the study of Jewish and Roman Law was the late Professor Boaz Cohen, who had edited a collection of articles on the subject titled "Jewish and Roman Law: A Comparative Study in Two Volumes". In the article "Questio Quid Iuris? – Some Thoughts on Jewish Law", published in the Harvard Theological Review 61:1 (1968), my father explained the significance of that two volume work.

My father wanted to study Jewish and Roman law at a very

advanced level, and he determined that the only way to do that would be to go to Oxford University in England. There was a professor, David Daube, who had published a number of works on comparative Jewish and Roman law, and he decided that Professor Daube would be the best person in the world to supervise his studies. My father used to tell me that he didn't really want to travel to England to study the subject, but he realized that he needed to go there in order to achieve his goal.

Professor Adolf Berger

Prior to traveling to England to pursue his doctoral degree, my father took a course on Roman Law taught by Professor Adolf Berger at the City College of New York in 1960. This was about two years before Professor Berger passed away in April of 1962. My father was very lucky to have had the opportunity to study with him while he was still alive, and I remember my father speaking very highly of him.

Professor Berger was an expert on Roman Law, and among many other writings he wrote a comprehensive dictionary of Roman legal terms titled the "Encyclopedic Dictionary of Roman Law", published in 1953. I remember my father telling me how he used to walk with Professor Berger to and from the class and would discuss interesting issues in Roman law as well as other topics. He told me that Professor Berger was a survivor of World War Two and the Holocaust and had come to the United States as a refugee. He had a very difficult time making a living in the United States as a Professor of Roman law, since the academics in the USA didn't really appreciate the value of studying Roman law. This was understandable because the American legal system is primarily based on Common law, which involves studying and analyzing relevant court cases and their outcomes, rather than being based on a system of Codes. It was terrible to see such a great scholar struggling so much financially, since very few people appreciated his greatness. My understanding is that Columbia University found work for him to do, which helped supplement his income, and he was very grateful for this.

Thesis on Unjust Enrichment in Jewish and Roman Law

My father's thesis at Oxford University was on "Unjust Enrichment in Jewish and Roman Law". The thesis itself only addresses the similarities and differences between the Jewish Law and the Roman Law as they relate to the topic of Unjust Enrichment. No attempt was made in the thesis to determine any possible influences between the two legal systems, which is a much more difficult thing to do.

Celebrating Sukkot in Oxford

One year when we were living in Oxford, my father decided to hire a carpenter to build a Sukkah in the back yard of the house that we were living in at the time. I think he told the carpenter that we needed a garden shed of some kind. He tried to explain to the carpenter that the structure needed to be somewhat unstable and not too strong, because the Jewish custom is to build the Sukkah as a semi-flimsy structure. The point is that the Sukkah is supposed to represent the huts that the Jews built when they were living in the wilderness, after having been liberated from Egypt by God. And those huts were not very strong. The carpenter ended up building it, but he wasn't happy creating a structure that wasn't up to his usual high standards.

Poem Composed in Oxford

I discovered this poem that my father wrote while studying and preparing his thesis on comparative Jewish and Roman Law at Oxford University:

"Going Crazy by Degrees"

Of Canada I've lots to say
Since there I first got my B.A.

But in New York I then was trained
And as a rabbi was ordained.

The Hebrew tongue I know quite well
Because I am an M.H.L.

In Greek and Latin I'm O.K.
Enough to get me my M.A.

Education's fine with me –
I've got an M.A. from T.C.

Though Roman Law is quite a pill –
With Jewish Law it makes – D. Phil.

And U.S. Law won't bother me
If I will get an LL.B.
But that's not all, for who can tell?
I may yet get a D.H.L. !

What's a DPhil?

My father used to point out that his degree, which he obtained from Oxford University in England, is called a "Doctor of Philosophy", or DPhil for short. In the United States the equivalent degree is called a PhD, which is an abbreviation of the Latin phrase "Philosophiae Doctor". He would say that it's strange that in the United States where people speak English and not Latin that the degree would have a name that is a Latin phrase, while in England, where the study and use of Latin is more common, the degree has a name that is a simple English phrase. It is interesting to note that the text of my BA degree from Columbia College in New York City is completely in Latin. Perhaps American universities have a predilection for Latin because it imparts a sense of respectability and authority.

After Oxford

After my father came back to New York City, having received his doctorate degree at Oxford University in 1965, he applied some of the teaching techniques and style that he had experienced in England to his classes at JTS. One of his students who studied with my father in the early 1970's told me that my father offered a course in the Oxford University "tutorial style" on the topic of Comparative Jewish, Christian, Muslim and Roman Law. The word tutorial comes from the word tutor, which in England has slightly different meaning than in the USA. In this tutorial style, the student would study a subject by reading books written by famous authors with different points of view over the course of a whole year, and then write essays on their research.

Another thing that would happen every year after my father

received his DPhil degree was his marching in the graduation ceremonies at JTS. He would wear his special red and blue robe that he received from Oxford University, and that indicated that he had graduated from Linacre College. I remember people being very impressed with the colorful robe, which really stood out from the simple black robes that most of the other professors wore.

Chapter 5

Jewish Divorce

Disclaimer: Please note that I am not a certified Get administrator or scribe, so the things that I am going to say in this section regarding Gittin should not be relied on as authoritative. If you have any questions about the rules of Gittin or about a specific Get, you should consult a specialist in the area of Jewish Divorce.

What's a Get?

A "Get" is a Jewish Divorce. The Torah says that if a man wants to divorce his wife, then he must write a document that says as much and give it to her. There are only a couple of verses in the Torah that relate to this law. The rest of the myriad of details regarding the laws of Jewish divorce are in the Mishnah and Talmud in the Tractate called Gittin, which is the plural of the word Get, as well as many books that have been written by rabbis over the years with clarifications about the laws and customs of Jewish divorce.

In Jewish law a man divorces his wife, and she accepts the divorce in front of witnesses, and not the other way around. It is similar to the process of Jewish marriage, which involves a man essentially telling a woman that he wants her to be his wife and the woman agreeing in front of witnesses to the proposal.

In the United States, Jewish divorces are normally not done unless there has already been a civil divorce, so that it is clear that the couple has definitely decided to terminate their marriage, and there is no possibility of them changing their minds. My father required that the civil divorce be final before starting to work on the Jewish divorce proceedings.

My father used to point out the difference between the Jewish and Christian views of divorce. From the Christian point of view, divorce is a sin. However, from the Jewish point of view it is a tragedy, but not a sin. Judaism recognizes that sometimes married couples are not able to live harmoniously together, and the Jewish divorce provides a legal way for the marriage to end.

One of the innovations that my father created at JTS was the process of Annulments of Jewish marriages, known in Hebrew as "Hafka'at Kiddushin". He developed the procedure and the wording of the certificate of Annulment which is issued as a result.

One of the problems that can arise when a Get is needed so that either the man or woman can get remarried Jewishly, is that either party could be recalcitrant, meaning that they refuse to cooperate. When this happens, an Annulment can be explored. The basic idea of an Annulment is that if the original marriage was done incorrectly, such that it is not really a valid Jewish marriage, then it can be declared to never have happened, and then a Jewish divorce is not needed at all. However, in order to issue an Annulment, a thorough investigation is needed to determine whether or not it is justified. If the investigation reveals that the original Jewish marriage was done correctly, then an Annulment won't be issued.

Boaz Cohen

Professor Boaz Cohen, of blessed memory, was the main person at JTS who prepared Gittin at the time that my father arrived on the scene. But he was not a scribe. He hired other people who were trained as Gittin scribes to do the actual writing. My father learned how to do that, using a feather and ink, and eventually became the main Gittin scribe for Professor Cohen. Boaz Cohen had a sort of monopoly on the preparation of Gittin within the New York City area. However, if someone needed a Get outside of the city, then my father was allowed to travel to that city and administer the Get. Eventually, when Professor Cohen got older and was no longer able to administer Gittin, my father took over that role in addition to the role of scribe.

It is very unusual for the Messader Gittin (administrator) to also be the Sofer (scribe), since one needs special training to be a Gittin scribe. Jewish scribes who write Torahs, Tefillin and Mezuzot (called "Sofer STAM" in Hebrew) are not qualified to write Gittin, unless they receive additional training specific to writing Gittin. My father was one of those rare individuals who was a master Gittin scribe and Messader Gittin.

Paper Size

Originally my father wrote Gittin using 8.5 x 11 inch paper, and eventually moved to writing Gittin using larger paper, which makes it much easier to write the letters using a feather pen. There is no requirement to write a Get using very small pieces of paper. If a larger piece of paper is easier to use, then it's fine. The main requirement for the paper is that it be taller than it is wide. So, for example, a square piece of paper should not be used, nor should a Get be written in "landscape" mode.

The Freedom Writer

My father used to say that he was a "Freedom Writer", because he wrote Gittin which liberated people from Jewish marriages that had gone bad. This term was a play on words that was meant to sound similar to the term "Freedom Rider", which was a term that referred to certain civil rights activists in the early 1960's.

People's Reactions to Needing a Get

I remember hearing discussions that my father had on the phone with people who needed a Get. Apparently, many Jews in the United State are completely unaware that if they are divorced by means of a civil decree issued by a secular court, they are still required to obtain a Jewish Get before marrying someone else who is Jewish. People would try arguing with my father and ask why it's necessary to go through the whole process of a Jewish divorce after they went through the whole process of obtaining a civil divorce. My father would have to explain to them that the law is the law, and that it is part of the Jewish tradition that a civil divorce is not enough, and that the laws and procedures relating to Gittin have been developed and formalized over thousands of years. Even though some of the things that need to be done might seem overly complicated or irrelevant, nevertheless they are required by Jewish law and therefore need to be done.

Names in a Get

One of the most important aspects of a Get involves writing the names of the husband and wife in the correct way. There are many rules relating to the names of the people who are mentioned in the text of the Get, and a whole book could be written on this topic alone. My father used to spend a lot of time researching Jewish names, including what their origins were and how to spell them correctly using Hebrew letters. It takes many years to become an expert at Jewish names, and my father used to say that he learned new things about names every year. There are certain principles that pertain to writing Jewish people's names in the Get, but inevitably a couple will come along where one or both of the parties have names that present some unique difficulties and require serious thought before deciding how to write their names correctly.

In addition to names of the people being divorced, the Get needs to contain the name of a river that is nearby, in order to help identify which city the Get was written in. One time, my father had travelled to Houston TX to write a Get, and it turned out that the nearest river was the Buffalo Bayou, which runs through the middle of Houston. My father asked someone there how the word "Bayou" in the name Buffalo Bayou is pronounced by the people in that area. The person said, "Rabbi, it's just like when two people meet, and one says to the other 'How's by you?'"

Some Common Misconceptions

A common misconception is that only the husband can "initiate" the process of obtaining a Get. This is not correct. Either the husband or the wife can initiate a Get because initiating a Get merely involves contacting a rabbi to get the process started. Once the rabbi has been contacted, then that rabbi will probably refer the case to another rabbi who is an expert in the area of Jewish divorce, since only a small fraction of rabbis have the specialized knowledge and training to prepare a Get themselves. It doesn't really matter who made the first move to contact a rabbi. What does matter is whether the husband is willing to agree to give his wife, who has already received a civil divorce, a Get. And it makes things a lot easier if the wife agrees to receive the Get.

Another common misconception about Gittin is the number of lines of text that the Get must contain. The Get is traditionally written with 12 lines of text, followed by two lines containing the signatures of witnesses. There is even a nice numerical calculation that the Tosafot commentary provides in the Talmud at the very beginning of Masechet Gittin, which says that the Hebrew letters that form the word Get have the total numerical value of 12 (Gimmel has the value three, and Tet has the value nine9), and that is why there are 12 lines of text.

However, my father used to point out that there are examples of Gittin from long ago that have been found in various archives where the number of lines exceeded 12. It appears that at some point in time the number of lines was fixed at 12, however in ancient times Gittin were sometimes written with more than 12 lines.

An interesting question arises: What if a Gittin scribe wrote a Get with more than 12 lines, perhaps because he ran out of space within the originally planned 12 lines. Is it a valid Get? The answer seems to be that it is not the best way to write the Get, and should be avoided as much as possible. However, if it was necessary to do so and there wasn't time to do it over and try to squeeze all of the words into 12 lines, and assuming that everything else about the Get is done correctly, then it would be considered valid.

The above scenario is an example of a whole area of Jewish law relating to Gittin. Namely, which things must be done a certain way when writing a Get, and if not done that way then the Get is considered invalid no matter what the circumstances are; and which things should ideally be done a certain way, but if they aren't then the Get is still considered valid. My father used to explain that there are many things that should be done a certain way when writing a Get, but if they are not done exactly that way then the Get is still considered valid. However, Gittin scribes should always try as hard as possible to do things the generally accepted way for the following reason: If someone needs to review a Get to make sure that it is valid, and one or more things are noticed that technically are acceptable after the fact, but should have been done differently, then it will make the reviewer wonder whether the Gittin scribe knew what they were doing, and whether there might possibly be other problems with the validity of the Get. So, it's always best to ensure that everything is done the generally accepted way when writing a Get.

Another common misconception about Gittin regards the use of a Shaliach, or agent, to deliver the Get to the wife. There are many people who believe that introducing an agent into the process causes all sorts of problems and therefore they should not be used. However, as my father used to point out, the Talmud in Tractate Gittin begins with a discussion of agents and what they are required to say when they deliver a Get. The fact that there is such an involved discussion about this topic implies that using a Shaliach to deliver a Get was a normal, and common, occurrence two thousand years ago.

Another common misconception relates to the Agunah problem. The word Agunah means "chained", and it refers to a wife who is unable to obtain a Get from her husband either because he refuses to give her one or because his whereabouts are unknown, and it is not clear whether he is still alive. If it can be proved that a husband died, then no Get is needed. Many people tend to regard the Agunah problem as just a women's issue. However, there are some men whose wife refuses to receive the Get. There are other situations where a wife is mentally incapable of receiving the Get because she is not able to understand what it is or what she is going to do after receiving the Get. These cases result in the husband becoming an Agun (the male form of the Hebrew word), and there is much less attention paid to the plight of Jewish men who are not able to divorce their wives via a Get.

Another misconception relates to the material that is used to write the Get. Some people think that a Get is, or should be, written on parchment, which is animal skin. However, a Get is always written on paper. The paper needs to be thick enough to allow the scribe to create ruled lines using a bone folder, and for the ink to penetrate the paper without showing through on the other side. Gittin used to be written on parchment a long time ago, but at some point in history the cost of parchment became so high and hard to find that some Gittin scribes started using paper as an affordable substitute. Even though parchment eventually became more affordable and more readily available, rabbis did not go back to using parchment in order not to disparage any Gittin that were written on paper. In other words, if rabbis started writing Gittin on parchment again, then it would raise suspicions that the Gittin that were written on paper were not done correctly.

How NOT to Negotiate the Fee for a Get

There are various costs involved to administer, write, and deliver a Get. There are the costs of the raw materials, such as the paper and ink, and there are fees that need to be paid to the witnesses and scribe (assuming that a separate scribe needs to be hired), not to mention the time spent by the rabbinical adminstrator. Because of all of these costs, a fee is normally charged for the Get.

One time a husband decided that he was going to negotiate with my father regarding the fee for the Get, the goal being to reduce the amount of the fee. The negotiation went something like this:

My father: There is a fee of $400 for the Get.

Husband: You say that there is a fee of $400? How about I only pay $300?

My father: OK, now the price is $500.

Husband: Wait, you just said that the price was $400.

My father: Now it's $600.

Husband: Hold on now, I'm negotiating with you, and you should be bringing the price down, not up.

My father: $700.

Husband: What??

My father: Well, if you stop "negotiating", we can do the Get at the price that I first mentioned, namely $400.

Husband: OK, $400 is fine with me.

Chapter 6

Life as a Scholar

Be Careful What You Say to a Scholar

I recall wanting to impress my father. when I was fairly young, with how I was learning new words at school. I had come across the word garrulous, which I thought meant "talkative". My father liked to talk about things, and one time when we were sitting at the kitchen table, I told him that he was garrulous. Well, that wasn't a good thing to do. It turns out that the word garrulous has a negative connotation of being excessively talkative; and not just talking a lot, but talking a lot of nonsense. My father got upset with me for saying that, at which point I realized that in the future I would need to fully understand all of the shades of meaning of a new word before using it at home.

The Proper Way to Handle Books

Before the invention of eBooks and audio books, there were just printed books that would sit on bookshelves. If you wanted to acquire a large number of books, you needed to have a lot of shelf space to store them. There are a number of things that my father used to tell me about the proper way to handle books in order to make them last longer, and to keep them in good condition so that the next person who would acquire the books would be able to enjoy using them.

My father did not approve of the practice of writing inside books, either to underline certain words or sentences, or to highlight words and sentences using a highlighter pen. There are many people who say that writing one's own notes inside a book is a good idea, and that it helps the reader to think about what is written in the book. However, my father felt that this practice just ended up damaging the book and making it harder for the next person to enjoy reading it.

Another thing that he used to point out is that there is a correct way and an incorrect way to take a book off a shelf. Many people will put their finger on the top of a book's spine and try to pull the book off the shelf by pulling on the top of the spine of the book. This is not a good practice, since doing so will inevitably end up damaging the spine of the book. A much better is to hold the book from both sides and pull it out that way.

He also used to explain the correct way to turn pages in a book so as to avoid damaging the paper by accidentally ripping it. A lot of people will try to turn a page in a book by putting their fingertip either at the top or at the bottom of a page, somewhere

… in the middle of the edge of the paper, and then pulling on the page to turn to the next page. The problem with this method is that one is likely to end up ripping the paper of the page. A much better way to turn a page is to first get one's finger underneath the page by lifting either the top or bottom corner of the page, and then gently turning the page by moving the hand while the finger is underneath the page.

One more thing that he used to say is that one should avoid putting books on a shelf that is exposed to direct sunlight. The ultraviolet light rays in the sunlight will eventually fade the colors on the spine of the book, which will reduce its resale value and just make it harder to read the title of the book that is printed on the spine. Something that I have noticed as I've gotten older is that I can identify books very easily by their spine: the colors, the font used for the title, the width of the spine, the material used to make the covers of the book. If a book's spine gets faded due to direct exposure to the sun, it can make it more difficult to locate a book on the shelf this way.

In addition to the goal of keeping the books in good shape, my father also emphasized the importance of treating books with respect. He said two things in regard to this aspect of book handling. First, he said that a book should be placed face up on the table until you are able to put it back on the shelf. Second, you should not leave a book open on the table while you walk away. Rather, you should put a bookmark in the book and close it until you return to continue reading. Both of these actions show a certain level of respect for the books, and are especially important if you are handling books of a religious nature.

Putting Books Back on the Shelf

When I was young and living at home, I remember my father telling me that if I wanted to read any of the many books in his library that I was welcome to do so any time. However, I had to agree to put the book back on the shelf when I was done using it. Of course, this advice pertains to printed books that sit on shelves, and does not pertain to eBooks and audio books that are totally electronic. When my father was studying to become a rabbi and scholar, eBooks and audio books did not exist. And they didn't exist for most of his career.

Looking Up Words in the Dictionary

Another thing my father used to tell me was "If you see a word that you don't understand or don't know the meaning of, look it up in the dictionary". This is an important scholarly habit, because there are always words, or phrases, that one encounters during one's studies and it is important to know exactly what those words mean. Before moving on to trying to understand the meaning of an entire sentence, you first need to understand the meanings of all of the words in the sentence.

Studying Word Origins

My father used to emphasize the importance of knowing what the origin of a word is. Knowing the etymology of a word, as it is called, helps one to understand the meaning of the word. Regarding "folk etymologies", which are popular explanations of how a word or phrase got its meaning, he would say that if more than one folk etymology of a word exists, then probably none of them is correct.

He would say that if one is trying to read a sentence in Hebrew that is difficult to understand, then one should focus on each word first and try to understand their meanings. After getting an idea of what each word means, then one should try to understand what the entire sentence means, and hopefully clearly understand the meaning that the author intended.

Common Mispronunciations

My father used to point out common mispronunciations. One of them was the word "pronunciation" itself. He would say that a lot of people say the word as though it were spelled "pronounciation". The related verb is "pronounce", but the noun is "pronunciation".

Another word that a lot of people say incorrectly, and which annoyed my father whenever he heard it said that way, is "memento". Many people commonly mispronounce that word as though it were spelled "momento". Probably people who make this error think that they are referring to something that helps you to remember a certain "moment" in time, but that is incorrect.

To Ask or Not To Ask?

There are times in one's career as a rabbi or Jewish scholar when a question arises and one needs to decide whether to research the question oneself, or reach out to a colleague or more senior rabbi or scholar for help. There seem to be those who feel that one should never ask others for help, and just apply the skills learned at the Yeshiva, Seminary or University where one was trained. There also appear to be others who don't mind being asked questions, and are always happy to help. The Jewish tradition encourages the asking of questions, so it seems to go a little against the tradition to not want to answer people's questions. I suppose it depends on the situation, who is doing the asking, what the topic is, and so on.

Among my father's papers I found a letter that he wrote to a college student who had asked him for some help with studying a certain topic. I don't know whether that response was typical, or whether the way that the person asked for help was the determining factor in his response. In any case, my father responded by encouraging the student to do their own research and try to answer their questions on their own. He wrote:

"In your study of the subject of ... you should receive sufficient guidance from your teachers and from materials available in your college library. Independent research is an exercise whose joys and achievements cannot be experienced vicariously. I have no doubt that you will find all you are seeking and much more by working on your own."

Read Multiple Books on a Subject

My father used to say that if one wants to study a particular subject, it's good to read more than one book on the topic because each author covers a little bit different material and approaches the topic with a slightly different point of view. Each book will add something new to one's understanding and knowledge.

Translation Errors

My father used to say that a common mistake among modern

translators of ancient Jewish texts is to translate the Hebrew word "Ner" as "candle". In fact, the word "Ner" refers to an oil lamp. Wax candles were an invention of the Middle Ages and did not exist at the time of the writing of the Mishnah and Gemara.

A common mistake is to translate the Biblical Hebrew word "Nefesh" as "soul". This is not correct. The word "Nefesh" means a person's physical body. There is a different Hebrew word, "Neshamah", which means one's soul.

Another Hebrew word that gets mistranslated a lot is "Olam", which can mean "world", but also has the meaning of "forever". The meaning of "forever" comes from the root for the word Olam which means "to forget". My father explained that if one can imagine a time that is so far in the future that nothing exists anymore, and all is forgotten, then that is the idea of "forever". There is a Hebrew hymn called "Adon Olam" that is sung at the end of the Shabbat morning services. In that context it means "Eternal Lord" (Adon means Lord), and not "Lord of the Universe" as it is often mistranslated. The succeeding verses of that song, which talk about God existing in the past, existing now and always existing in the future, support the translation of "Eternal Lord".

The Hebrew word "Sofer" is commonly translated as "scribe", but when it was used in the Mishnah about 2,000 years ago, it just meant "teacher". There is a Mishnah in Tractate Gittin (Chapter 3, Mishnah 1) which is a good example of this. It says "If someone is walking in the marketplace, and hears the voice of the Soferim (plural form of the word Sofer) calling out Mr. So-and-so is divorcing his wife so-and-so ...". A common translation of the word Soferim is Scribes, but in this context it just means the teachers in a school for children who are learning to read and write Hebrew. The teachers would use the text of a Get (Jewish divorce document) as an exercise for the students to learn how to write Hebrew and Aramaic letters and words.

Another translating mistake that my father used to point out is the translation of the Hebrew words "Ad Shakamti Devorah" in the poem called Shirat D'vorah in Hebrew, or "The Song of Deborah" (Judges 5:7). That phrase is sometimes translated as "Until I arose, Deborah!", and some people use this translation to denigrate Deborah by claiming that she was being self-centered and egotistical in her statement. But it really should be translated as "Until you, Deborah, arose" and was spoken by someone other than Deborah herself. The explanation is that the ending of the word "Shakamti", that is the last vowel "i", is actually an ancient grammatical form that is the same as the second person singular. That special ending also appears in a few places in the Psalms, and can be used as an indicator of which Psalms are of very ancient origin, because that special word ending stopped being used at some point.

Another common mistranslation is calling the sea creature that swallowed Jonah a whale. In fact, according to the original Hebrew text, the creature was a giant fish. A whale is a mammal, and a fish is definitely not a mammal.

Another word that is commonly mistranslated is the word "Bonayich" in the paragraph that is said at the end of the morning services in the synagogue on Shabbat. The paragraph is a quote from the Talmud (Brachos 64a), which says that the word Banayich (your children) should be read Bonayich. And most people translate Bonayich to mean "Your builders". My father used to say that the word Bonayich comes from the Hebrew root BNH which means "to understand". So, what it means is "those who try to understand Your teachings".

Scholars and Scholarship

My father had a certain disdain for people who professed to be scholars, but who probably didn't deserve to be called true scholars. One of the things he used to say was "Taking a simple idea and making it overly complicated is Scholarship; taking a complicated idea and making it simple is Genius". When he read or heard the comments of someone who purported to be a scholar, but who in his opinion was not, he would say that the person was a "Talmid Chucham Foon Dee Mah Nishtanah". This is a Yiddish phrase which could be translated as "A scholar among the nursery school kiddies". He also liked to use the pun "Talmid Hokum" (using the English slang word "Hokum" instead of the Hebrew word "Chacham") to refer to someone who acted as though they were a great scholar, but who in reality was just an average person (a "fake" scholar).

My father used to say that one aspect of genius is being able to take a complex subject and describe it in a simple way. In other words, if a certain topic is very complex, then a genius will be able to figure out a way to describe it in simple terms so that anyone who is not an expert in that field will be able to get the basic idea and understand it at a fundamental level. This is also the idea behind the Cynics who believed that one test of a statement's veracity is whether or not it can be explained in simple terms, "while standing on one foot."

Aramaisms

My father used to talk about something called "Aramaisms". These are grammatical forms that appear in Hebrew texts that appear to be Aramaic, but are really just "imitations" of Aramaic grammatical forms.

Poetry

My father used to enjoy reciting the following poem:

> The more your learn, the more you know.
> The more you know, the more you forget.
> The more you forget, the less you know.
> So, why study at all?

In one of my father's lectures I heard him say the following about how NOT to split words in poetry. He quoted the following German poem:

> Hans Saks war ein shoe-
> macher und poet datsu.

Translation as written: "Hans Saks was a shoe, maker and a poet also". The intended meaning is "Hans Saks was a shoemaker, and a poet also". The lesson to be learned is, be careful where you split words within poetry.

Meanings of Various Hebrew Words

Meaning of the word Cheit

My father used to point out that the word Cheit is usually

translated as "sin". However, the word originally comes from an archery term meaning to "miss the mark". So, when the word Cheit is used to mean "sin", what it really means is that a person has missed the mark in his or her life, and has not acted properly.

Meaning of the word Olam

The Hebrew word Olam originally comes from a root that means to forget. So, how does that word come to mean "forever"? The answer is that if one thinks about what the world will be like many years in the future, so far in the future that people won't exist anymore, then one will realize that everything that has happened in the world will have been forgotten. There won't be anyone left to remember anything. That is how it means "forever".

There is a related Hebrew expression, "Chai Olamim", that appears a number of times in the daily prayer services, and is used to describe one of the aspects of God. My father used to point out that it is commonly mistranslated as "Life of the Universe". The Hebrew word Chai means life, and Olam can mean "universe". However, when that expression is used in the prayers it means "The One Who lives eternally".

Special meaning of the word Va'Yigva

My father used to point out that the word Va'Yigva in the Torah in Genesis 25:8, which is used to mean that Abraham "died", has a special meaning. It implies that a person has lied down and is stretched out and relaxed, when they pass away. So the Torah is trying to say that when Abraham died, he did so in a very relaxed way and was able to pass away feeling satisfied that he had lived a good life. That word is an example of a word that has a special shade of meaning that is easy to miss if one isn't reading the text very carefully.

Derivation of the word Benching

A lot of people are probably not aware what the word "benching", which refers to the "Grace After Meals" recited after a meal, comes from. It is derived from the Latin verb benedictere, meaning "to bless".

The Title Rabban

If you study the rabbinical writings, including the Mishnah, Gemara, and Midrashim, you will encounter various Hebrew terms that mean "rabbi", such as "Rav" and "Rabbee". There is a special term of great honor for a rabbi called "Rabban", and it is used to refer to a person who is not only a great rabbi within the Jewish community, but also a person who interfaces with the secular government as a representative of the Jewish people. So, it is both a rabbinical term and a political term. One famous example is Rabban Shimon Ben Gamliel, who lived at the time of the destruction of the Second Temple and is quoted in the Mishnah.

Derivation of the word Cholent

The word Cholent (or sometimes pronounced Chulnt), is a Yiddish word that refers to the hot slow-cooked meal that is prepared before Shabbat, begins cooking before sundown on a Friday night, and is eaten for lunch on Saturday. My father used to explain that the word comes from the French word for hot, "chaude". Ashkenazic Jews call this dish Chulent, and Sephardic Jews call it Chamin, which literally means "hot things" in Hebrew. It makes sense that Ashkenazic Jews would have used a French word to refer to this dish, since France was a major center of Ashkenazic Jewry during the middle ages.

Things that Irked My Father

There were a number of things that people would say that irked my father whenever he heard them. One of those things was the expression "to bring down" which is used by some people to mean "to quote". He used to say that it sounds like you are talking about shooting down an airplane or something like that. The scholarly way to say this is to use the verb "to quote", meaning that you are repeating something that you read or heard in the name of someone else. Probably the words "to bring down" are a literal translation of a Yiddish phrase that means the same thing, however it is not proper English usage.

The way that people use the "thumbs up" sign to mean "Yes" in a positive sense used to annoy my father. He would explain that the origin of the thumbs up hand sign was the gladiator fights in the amphitheater in ancient Rome. After a long battle, the fighter who was still standing would look up at the Emperor and ask whether or not to kill the defeated fighter, who was lying on the ground. The Emperor would indicate his answer by either pointing his thumb up, meaning "Yes, go ahead and kill him", or pointing his thumb down, meaning "No, don't kill him."

Another grammatical error that a lot of people make is what my father called "qualifying the absolute", meaning that you are trying to apply an adjective to a noun that cannot be qualified. For example, some people say that something is "more correct", "more perfect", or "more unique" than something else. The reason this is incorrect from a grammatical standpoint is that either something is correct or not correct, and something is either perfect or not perfect.

Another phrase that people say which really annoyed my father was "Canadian Geese", when they were referring to the species of goose called the "Canada Goose". The plural of Canada Goose is Canada Geese, not Canadian Geese.

Another irksome phrase was "first annual", referring to the first event in a series of annual events. A lot of people tend to do this. When someone comes up with an idea for a new event, and they want to make it sound like it's going to continue happening year after year, they announce it as the "first annual" such-and-such event. The problem with saying this is that the word "annual" implies that something has been happening already a year prior. After the second event is held a year after the first event, one can correctly say that it is the "second annual" whatever. But, when one is talking about the first event of a certain kind, you can't correctly call it the first annual event until you have at least one more of its kind the following year.

One thing that especially irked my father was when people put a dot on their capital I's. When I was a young student in elementary school, my father attended a science fair that the school had put on. There was a sign at the fair that said, "SCIENCE FAIR" spelled using all capital letters, but the capital I's were dotted. My father pointed this out to one of the teachers at the fair. After listening to my father's comment, the teacher responded that my father was being "too picayune". Apparently, those dots on the capital I's were something that my father never forgot, because I remember hearing the story a good number of times.

My father really didn't like it when people would tell him that they wanted to "pick his brain". He thought that it sounded very aggressive, almost violent, and just plain not nice. If someone wants to ask someone else some questions, do they really have to make it sound like bodily injury to their head will be involved?

Another thing that my father used to point out is that a lot of people confuse the words "smell" and "stink". If one wants to say that something has a foul odor, one should say that it stinks. If one wants to say that a person can detect odors easily, then you should say that they have a good sense of smell.

One other pair of words that a lot of people frequently mix up is "infer" and "imply". People infer things logically based on hearing or reading something. People imply things when they say or write something and whatever they said or wrote suggests something else.

Chapter 7

Father and Friend

Playing Games

When I was a child, there were a couple of games that I liked to play, and I tried to get my father to play them with me. One was chess. The other was a hockey game that was played on a board with sliding rods to control the players and a small plastic net on either end. I remember that once I got good enough at either game to beat my father, he stopped wanting to play those games with me.

Looking back on it, I think it would have been nicer if he had played with me even though he would have lost most, if not all, of the time. It would have created a greater bond between us. I highly recommend to any parent who has a child who wants to play some game with you, and you know that you will probably lose most of the time, just go ahead and play with your child anyway. The years go by quickly, and before you know it, they won't want to play those children's games anymore. If you don't play with them, you will miss out and possibly regret it for many years afterward.

Mathematics

Although my father was very smart and excelled in many academic subjects, mathematics was not one of his strong areas. He was definitely more of a liberal arts person, and not an engineer. However, he did understand some mathematical ideas, including the concept of a mathematical sequence. One of the riddles that he used to like to tell was this: What is the next number in the following sequence? 14, 32, 42, 72.

The answer is 96. Why? Because those numbers are the street numbers of the stations on the 7th Avenue Express subway in Manhattan heading northbound. If you are a Manhattan person, you probably got the answer pretty easily. Otherwise, you probably didn't.

Running Home

One Shabbat morning, I went to the prayer service at JTS. At some point I realized that my father was not there, and I tried to find out why. Someone told me that he wasn't feeling well and had to stay home. When I heard that, I immediately ran out of the building and ran home as quickly as I could in order to make sure that my father was all right. The security guard, who was stationed inside the front gates of the building, later told me that he had never seen me run so fast. I wasn't an athletic child, and running wasn't my thing. In fact, most children my age could walk faster than I could run. But apparently, on that day, I found the strength to run home quickly and check on my father. I think he was surprised, but happy, to see me.

Ask, My Son

My father used to like to use the Hebrew phrase "Sh'al B'ni" (ask, my son) if I said that I had a question. This phrase probably comes from the story recorded in the Gemarah in Tractate Shabbat 31a, in which Hillel is approached by someone who wanted to ask him annoying questions. Of course, in my case, I actually was his son. So, the phrase was very appropriate.

Bird Sounds

My father used to like hearing the sounds made by the Mourning Dove, which is pictured on the cover of this book. He used to mention it whenever he heard the sounds, and he would imitate them: oo-OO-oo-oo-oo. Every now and then, usually when I am walking to the synagogue on a Shabbat morning, I hear the cooing of a mourning dove, and it makes me think of my father. The sound is comforting, and helps boost my sprits before starting the morning service. My advice to anyone reading this is to pay attention to your relatives or close friends when they tell you about a favorite bird of theirs. Learn what the bird sounds like when it calls. Then, after your relative or close friend has passed away, when you hear that bird sound it will remind you of them and it will bring you some comfort.

Calligraphy Course

One of the best memories I have of my father is taking a calligraphy course with him during the Summer of 1976 (the other one is sitting with him as a child during Shabbat morning services at JTS). What an amazing opportunity to learn traditional calligraphy with an accomplished Gittin scribe such as my father!

Of course, we used metal calligraphy pens and not feather pens. But it was a really enjoyable course, and looking back on it now after so many years, I realize that my father probably really enjoyed taking the class with me also.

Chapter 8

Adult Education Courses

My father served as rabbi and spiritual leader at the Shaare Zedek synagogue at 93rd Street and Broadway in Manhattan two times. The first time was in the early 1970's, and the second time was in the early 1980's. My Bar Mitzvah occurred while he was the rabbi in 1971, and this was an especially happy event for me.

While my father was serving as rabbi at Congregation Shaare Zedek, he gave adult education classes to the members of the synagogue on various Jewish topics. Some of the topics for the classes were:

- Maimonides, known in Hebrew as The Rambam
- Ethics of the Fathers, known in Hebrew as Pirkei Avot
- The Passover Seder
- Proverbs, known in Hebrew as Mishlei
- Psalms, known in Hebrew as Tehillim

In this chapter, I will include some of the thoughts and ideas that he expressed in those classes.

Maimonides

Maimonides, known by the Hebrew abbreviation "Rambam", was someone who was a product of his time, and yet was also very influential in his time. He also influenced later generations a great deal. The name Maimonides is the Greek form of the name which literally means "The son of Maimon". His Hebrew name was Moshe Ben Maimon. The abbreviation Rambam comes from the first letters of the words Rabbi Moshe Ben Maimon.

During his lifetime, Maimonides wrote an extremely large quantity of material. And he wrote all of that material while employed full-time as a physician. If one wanted to copy all of his writings by hand, it would probably take many years to do so. It was truly an amazing accomplishment.

The Rambam was born in Cordoba, Spain, in the year 1135, and died in Cairo, Egypt, in 1204, and did most of his writing in Egypt. However, whenever he refers to himself in his writings, he calls himself "HaSefaradi", meaning "The Spaniard". One of the characteristics, or themes, of the written works of Maimonides was to defend Judaism in the face of the Islamic religious world that surrounded him. The other major theme that one finds in his writings was to create a philosophy of Judaism which would be meaningful in the world of philosophy of that time where many of the Greek philosophers were discovered, especially Aristotle. The Arab and Muslim philosophers of that time were very heavily dependent on Aristotle, and one finds that Maimonides needed to defend Judaism against many of the teachings of Aristotle.

My father used to say that the Rambam was a Yekke, because he was extremely well organized, logical and precise in his writings.

Adult Education Courses

The term "Yekke" is a word that refers to German Jews who were known for being especially exact and precise in their activities. An excellent example of this aspect of his writings is his legal work called the Mishneh Torah, which organizes all of Jewish law into 14 large sections or books, and within those books into very well-organized sections.

The Hebrew book title Mishneh Torah, which means "The Second Edition of the Torah", comes from the expression "Mishneh HaTorah Hazot" in Deuteronomy 17:18, where the book of Deuteronomy is depicted as a recapitulation of the laws that are mentioned in the first four books of the Torah.

The Mishneh Torah was a very controversial work when it was written, and for many years afterwards. The Mishneh Torah does not mention any details regarding the basis for any of its legal statements. Many rabbis didn't approve of this approach because they felt that it was important to explain how each legal statement was derived from the traditional textual sources and the subsequent statements and comments from great rabbis over the centuries.

My father used to explain that those rabbis missed the whole point of the Mishneh Torah. The target audience of the work was not the rabbis, but rather the ordinary Jew who has to work for a living and has very little time to study all of the sources and legal arguments, and just wants to know what the Jewish law is in various situations that are encountered in daily life. It was very difficult for the average Jew to get a good education at that time due to the lack of schools that people could afford to send their children. In addition, most people are not legal scholars, and including all of that material would serve little purpose other than to confuse the readers in the target audience. Finally, Maimonides realized that many of the writings of the rabbis who commented on the Jewish law were contained in many books (manuscripts, actually) which were very difficult to obtain and to get a full understanding of the totality of Jewish law as it pertained to the average person. The Mishneh Torah was written by Maimonides in order to provide for the average Jew a simple statement of what it is that a Jew should do to live as a Jew.

The Mishneh Torah was written in Hebrew, even though most of the Rambam's writings, including his commentary on the Mishnah which he wrote when he was young, and his major philosophical work known as the "Guide for the Perplexed" which he wrote when he was much older, were written in Arabic. Also, many philosophical works were written in Arabic at that time, and because of that Maimonides felt that it was appropriate to write a work of philosophy, even though it was Jewish philosophy, in Arabic. The reason why Maimonides wrote the Mishneh Torah in Hebrew rather than Arabic was to make the Mishneh Torah easily accessible to Jews all over the world who could read Hebrew, but most of whom could not read Arabic.

Frequently, people who study the Mishneh Torah of the Rambam will say that a certain part of the book is "difficult", or they will say that it is a "difficult Rambam". When they say this, they don't mean that it is hard to understand what the Rambam said, since he wrote in a very simple and easy-to-understand Hebrew. What they mean is that it is difficult to understand how the Rambam derived his conclusion on a particular point of law from the various sources in the Mishnah and Talmud.

Pirkei Avot

The Chapters of the Fathers, known in Hebrew as Pirkei Avot, is a section of the Talmud, actually part of the Mishnah. Contrary to popular belief, it is not a moral code. Rather it is a collection of highly specialized statements. Pirkei Avot has two purposes: The first is a description of the Oral Law, known in Hebrew as the "Torah She'b'al Peh", and how it came about. The Oral Law is the one that Judges need to apply when deciding cases that are brought before them. So, Pirkei Avot contains advice to Judges, such as greeting all people who come before you with friendliness, being fair in judgement, and so on. Basically, how to apply the Torah correctly and what constitutes proper conduct for Judges. The second purpose is to teach how to learn the Torah, including ideas relating to how to be a good student, for example.

One of the statements relating to being a good student is the one made by the famous Rabbi Hillel, quoted in Pirkei Avot 2:5, who used to say that the shy person won't learn. In Hebrew the saying is "Lo ha'bayshan lameid". My father expounded that this phrase is referring to more than just a shy person, who is timid and afraid to ask questions. It also refers to people who are very knowledgeable about a subject, but are afraid to ask questions in a classroom setting because they are afraid that they might not sound very intelligent. He provided the following real life example.

My father was sitting in a class at Teachers College at Columbia University and the professor was explaining a particular point regarding education. Part of his explanation included a reference, without explanation, to a concept that had been developed by a well-known expert in the field of education. My father was not familiar with that concept, and since nobody else raised their hand to ask for clarification, he decided to do so. The professor explained the concept in detail, and then asked the class whether everyone else was familiar with it. Nobody else seemed to know about it, but they were all afraid to ask. My father explained that this reluctance to ask questions was due to the students not wanting to appear ignorant in front of their classmates. The statement of Hillel in Pirkei Avot is trying to tell us that we should not worry about how knowledgeable or ignorant we might appear to others when we have a question.

The Passover Seder

Matzah

Why do we eat Matzah on the Jewish holiday of Passover? A reason is given in the Torah, that the Israelites were in such a rush to leave Egypt that the dough did not have time to rise, so they baked it quickly and it came out as Matzah and not as normal bread. My father used to give a different reason for the requirement, or Mitzvah, of eating Matzah on Passover. He used to say that one of the major accomplishments of ancient Egypt, a thing that they were known for and very famous for, was the discovery of yeast and the invention of baking bread where the dough rises due to the yeast. Since this was such a strong symbol of Egypt, the Torah commands us to avoid eating bread during the festival of Passover, in order to make it clear that we totally reject the culture and civilization of the ancient Egyptians, symbolized by the creation of yeast bread.

The Cup of Elijah

Why do we place a special empty cup on the Seder table during Passover, and why do we call it "The Cup of Elijah" in English, or "Kos Eliyahu" in Hebrew? Some people think, mistakenly, that we are putting it there so that Elijah the Prophet can visit our homes and drink some wine from the special cup, perhaps because he is thirsty after travelling around to everyone's home on Passover. My father explained that the reason for the special cup is as follows.

When the Torah, Exodus 6:6-7, describes the Exodus from Egypt, it uses several verbs to describe what God did to deliver the Jewish people from the slavery and bondage in ancient Egypt. There are four verbs of deliverance: "I will bring you out", "I will save you", "I will deliver you", and "I will take you". And it is because of these four verbs that we drink four cups of wine at the Passover Seder. Each cup represents one of the verbs of deliverance.

However, there is an opinion in the Talmud, attributed to Rabbi Tarfon, that there is a fifth verb of deliverance, "I will bring you" (to the Land of Israel) in Exodus 6:8. And because of this fifth verb, we should actually drink five cups of wine at the Seder. Since this is a disagreement that was never fully resolved, we have a custom to drink four cups of wine during the Seder, but we put out a fifth cup called the Cup of Elijah to symbolize the future resolution of this dispute by Elijah the Prophet, who will visit us during the time of the Mashiach (the Messiah).

Mishlei – The Book of Proverbs

There are three books in the Jewish Bible which are referred to by non-Jewish scholars as "wisdom literature". They are all in the third main section of the Bible known in Hebrew as K'tuvim, or Writings. The Hebrew names of the three books are Mishlei

("Proverbs"), Iyov ("Job"), and Kohelet ("Ecclesiastes"). These books are referred to as Judaism's "wisdom literature" because they are supposed to contain information that helps people to get along in the world. These books are not primarily religious books, in the sense of a prophet giving you a message from God. So, some questions have been raised: What is particularly Jewish about these three books? Where did they come from? And why are they in the Jewish Bible?

It is important to note that other nations and culture also have what is known as their "wisdom literature", one of the most famous being the ancient Greek wisdom literature. The other wisdom literatures generally contain information that people should know about how the world works, and good advice on how to succeed in the world.

The Greeks even had a special kind of wisdom literature that we call the Sophistic Literature. The Sophists in ancient Greece were like travelling professors, and their name comes from the Greek word "Sophos", which means knowledge. The Sophists would move around and teach wisdom in a very special way. They are mentioned in the Dialogues of Plato, and Plato himself was a kind of Sophist. The special thing that the Sophists did, in addition to teaching the standard wisdom material, was to train young men who wanted to become political leaders. In those days, a political leader meant a public speaker or orator. If you could get up in front of a large crowd and persuade the crowds to follow you, then that meant that you were a successful politician. The Sophists didn't focus mainly on the policies of the government, but rather on the techniques that are used to convince people to agree with you. Because of this, the Sophists got a bad name, and the term Sophistry came to mean being able to use clever arguments to prove any point that you wanted.

Two of our Jewish books of wisdom are very similar to the literature of the Sophists: Mishlei and Kohelet. Many of the statements in Mishlei start with the phrase "Sh'ma B'ni", which literally means "Listen, my son". But in the context of Mishlei, the author is not speaking to his son, rather the word "B'ni" just means "young man". The idea is that an older person, who has gained wisdom from experience, is teaching a younger person about the world and what it's like based on the older person's experience. Both of these books contain short statements of advice. The book of Job, on the other hand, is a single long essay on a very important topic: Why is there suffering in the world, and why is it that the people who obey the will of God and are basically good people suffer so much during their lives?

Let's consider why the book of Proverbs is called "Mishlei". The Hebrew word Mishlei is the plural form of the word Mashal, which in modern Hebrew is translated as a "parable", that is a story that illustrates a point. The English word parable comes originally from the word Greek word "parabole", which literally mean "throwing to the side", or figuratively means "going around", so it's a story that doesn't tell you the idea directly. With a parable, you listen to the story, and you get the point that is made by hearing the story.

However, back in the time of the writing of the book of Mishlei, the Hebrew word Mashal meant something else. It meant a teaching whose purpose was to help you understand how the world works, rather than stories that try to make a point. And that is why Mishlei is considered "wisdom literature", because it's goal is to make you smart. The thing that distinguishes Mishlei from the wisdom literature of other nations and cultures is that it emphasizes moral teachings, including what is important in the world, what is valuable, what are the things that one should do, and what are the things that one should watch out for. For example, watch out for con men who try to trick you into doing things that are harmful. In a nutshell, Mishlei provides moral education of a young person. On the other hand, it also includes a certain amount of practical ideas for success in the world. The reason that it also includes practical suggestions in addition to moral teaching is because it is intended to educate young people, and education naturally involves a certain amount of practical advice in addition to moral teaching.

Tehillim – The Psalms

There is a selection of Psalms near the beginning of the daily morning prayer service, known in Hebrew as "P'sukei D'zimrah", or Verses of Song. They are a kind of preliminary service that has the purpose of setting the mood for the rest of the service. The other main parts of the morning service are the Shema prayer and the Shmoneh Esrei or Tefillah.

Note that this collection of Psalms is known as Verses of Song, which according to some scholars implies that originally only individual verses were said, and not entire chapters. So, it appears to have been originally a collection of verses, probably a small collection which became bigger as time went on.

During the Shabbat morning service, additional Psalms are added to the collection that is said every day, starting with Psalm 19. Some scholars have said that Psalm 19 is the most beautiful one of them all. This Psalm is focused on nature. It doesn't speak of people or nations. There is nothing individualistic about it, rather it is very universal. It talks about nature, which can appeal to any person in any place.

The first verse, after the standard introductory verse, is structured using the "A, B, C, C, B, A" type of parallelism. It says, "The skies tell of the glory of God, and of the works of His hands speak the heavens". In the first half of the verse, A = "The skies", B = "tell", C ="of the glory of God". In the second half of the verse, C = "of the works of His hands", B = "speak", A = "the heavens".

The next verse says, "One day speaks to the other day, and one night speaks to the other night". The idea being conveyed here is that creation itself gives testimony to the greatness of the Creator of the world. The next verse, "There is no speaking and no words, and their voices are not heard", means that it is a kind of silent statement that the heavens, the sky and the earth make. That is, just by looking at the sky and the earth you get the message coming through, which they don't speak. The next verse, "Their message extends to the whole earth, and their words to the ends of the earth", reiterates this idea.

One time, my father was conducting High Holiday services in Gainesville, which is in Northen Florida. It's warm and colorful there, but not hot and steamy the way Southern Florida is. He had gotten up early to walk to the synagogue because the walk was fairly long. And as he walked, he saw and heard a collection of birds the like of which he had never seen before. The birds of Northern Florida are many, and varied in their colorful feathers and their musical sounds and songs. As he was walking along, the air was filled with birds and bird songs, and he was fascinated by this experience, because walking down Amsterdam

Avenue in Manhattan you don't hear that. When he arrived at the synagogue, he remarked to the members that this must be the meaning of the verse "The skies speak of the glory of God". He had never heard the sky speaking before, but that morning it sounded like the whole sky was speaking. The world is filled with various natural sounds that speak of the glory of God, not using words as humans do, but with various sounds that make up their own natural "language".

Chapter 9

Sermons

My father had the opportunity to serve as the rabbi at Congregation Shaare Zedek in Manhattan for a second time in the early 1980's. He was a very good sermonizer and kept his sermons short and to the point, which the congregation appreciated very much. He tended to focus on one big idea that related either to the Torah reading, current events, or the current Jewish holiday. He drew freely on the Talmud and Midrash for ideas, and was always thinking of the entire Jewish people, and not just those who lived in New York City or the United States. One of the most important ideas that he tried to communicate was the unity of the Jewish people.

I am including seven of his sermons here to give you a taste of what he used to say on regular Shabbat mornings (one sermon from each of the Five Books of the Torah), and one for each of the Jewish holidays of Pesach and Sukkot.

Sermon 1 – Shabbat Parashat Vayera – Genesis 18:1 to 22:24 (November 1981)

Today's Torah reading includes the scene of Abraham arguing with God about the fate of the city of Sodom. This was not just a "bargaining" event, although it could appear to be one. The rabbis of the Talmud see it as teaching universal principles. The arguments that Abraham makes are not purely regarding numbers of people, but also regarding other factors. For example, the number 10, which in Judaism equates to a Minyan, and which according to the rabbis represents a "core" or a basic group of a Jewish community. If there is no Minyan, then the community is already not really alive.

But the real argument that Abraham was making is that God has to understand the nature of the world that He has created. If it is perfect justice that He wants, then the world has no chance for survival. If you want a world, then you cannot have perfect justice. If you want perfect justice, then you cannot have a world. Also, God is trying to hold the rope at both ends. The analogy is that of trying to pull something with a rope. You have to tie one end of the rope around the thing that you are pulling, and you must only hold the other end. If you take both ends of the rope in your hands, you just end up defeating yourself.

Perfect justice is impossible, and God must relent.

On the other hand, we must strive for the highest standards possible. That is why the debate took place. Not because God did not know which sins were taking place in Sodom, but to teach us this principle.

Of all the applications of this principle, let us look to our religious institutions, the synagogue, the rabbis, the Torah, and our customs. If we look to them, and get the impression that they are not perfect, then we may be led to abandon them altogether, and that would be wrong.

We must remember that all human life is imperfect, even famous religious personalities are not perfect, and even the Synagogue is not perfect. But, nevertheless, there is much to be gained by learning from them, by participating, and by deriving the good that is there. And if we see imperfections, let us remember that we too are imperfect.

Then we can build a truly good community. Not a perfect one, but one that is truthful, constructive, and upholding the best traditions of our people. Amen.

Sermon 2 – Shabbat Parashat Yitro – Exodus 18:1 to 20:23 (February 1982)

The Revelation on Mount Sinai. The statement of the people that "We will do, and we will listen" has echoes in how Yitro, the father-in-law of Moses, pictured Moses as a leader.

The Great Midrash on Parashat Yitro says that individuals who spend their time focused on studying Torah, the "Chaverim", can ignore public issues and not suffer any punishment for doing so. However, when one becomes a leader, then you can no longer ignore the public and their concerns (Midrash Rabbah on Exodus, section 27:9).

When you become a leader, your fortunes are intertwined with the community. It is easy to criticize when one is not in a position of having to make decisions. We all do this with our leaders. If there is any problem we say that the government should be doing something about it. Crime, the economy, the condition of the cities, the poor, and so on. If the sports team plays poorly, we say "Fire the coach".

So, also, in Jewish religious life. If there is anything that can be complained about, it must be the fault of the leaders – the people who are the rabbis and the lay leadership. Yitro knew this, and told it to Moses. He even set up a system of bureaucrats to help with the work. But ultimately he knew that, in the words of Harry Truman, the buck would stop at the desk of Moses.

But the lesson of the Revelation at Mount Sinai was that the entire people were present, and heard the words of the Ten Commandments. In the words of the Talmud, "Even a housemaid at the Splitting of the Sea saw things that the Prophet Ezekiel never dreamed of". It is the responsibility of every Jew to live a Jewish life, and to be responsible for his conduct with respect to his fellow human beings, and with the world.

We are the descendants of those who said, "We will do, and we will listen". We, every one of us, will obey, and do, inasmuch as it is given to us to be able to lead a Jewish life, to lead a good life, to work for the upkeep of our communities, rather than to expect the community to work for us.

Our leaders cannot do more than to show us the way. That is the purpose of leadership. But the achievement is that of every individual person.

The Torah will live, and continue, not because of the "Chaverim", the criticizers, the private people whose only public activity is to find fault with the leaders, but because of those who give and work and build. And they are the ones who will have the satisfaction of knowing that their dedication will be passed on to the generations to come.

Sermon 3 – Parashat Vayikra – Leviticus 1:1 to 5:26 (March 1983)

Religious teaching comes from inspired teachers and thinkers. Inspiration is like creativity – something that comes to a person from the outside, from above, so to speak. But how does one get inspiration?

One of the greatest inventors of all time, Thomas Edison, is generally thought to have said, "Genius is one percent inspiration and 99 percent perspiration." Inspiration only comes to those who work very hard to get it.

But there is no clear or obvious way to achieve inspiration. The only way is to work at all of the ordinary things, to do all that one can to solve one's problems and questions with one's own resources. Them, perhaps, inspiration will come.

In our religious life, where do we get the inspiration to solve our problems? By not waiting for inspiration, but working at our task in any way we can, even in an uninspired way.

How does this relate to the Torah reading of today? Our inspiration comes from two sources: From God, who gives it to us in His good time, and from our own hard work and our concern for the people of Israel, when we experience the sacrifices of ordinary people.

We cannot withdraw into the world of study, and abstract ideas. Rather we must all be in each other's presence, to gain the true inspiration that will bring us to understand God's will. Then, our sacrifice will truly be an offering to God that is beautiful and acceptable.

Sermon 4 – Parashat Naso – Numbers 4:21-7:89 (June 1981)

The counting of the Jewish people, the Census. Why a Census? We will come back to this question.

Many peoples have had the custom of a general count of the population. Ancient Egypt, and pre-Israelite Canaan, for example. And the counting of the population generally served two purposes: taxation, and military levies and conscription.

In the Torah, two censuses are recorded: one at Sinai and the other in the plains of Moab as the Jews were about to enter the Promised Land. In later times, the census was necessary, but feared.

There was also a census in the time of King David. And there are mixed views of this event. In the Book of Samuel, it is stated that David did this at the command of God. But in the Book of Chronicles, it is thought to be the act of the Satan.

In modern times, a new element has been added to the need for a census: the need of a democratic representation in government. In the USA, the census is required every ten years to allocate the seats in the House of Representatives.

In our time, a new element has come about because there is so much money going from the Federal Government to the States and localities on the basis of population that it has become a matter of money. We are urged to be counted so that the City can get more Federal money. Even lawsuits have been instituted to require the Federal Government's Bureau of the Census to estimate the number of people each year because of the money going to the States.

But why did the Torah have a census? What reason did the rabbis attribute to the need for a census?

The people of Israel were counted because they are precious to God. That which one holds precious, one counts all the time. The miser counts his money, the athlete counts his trophies, and the stamp collector counts his stamps. And we are so few, and so important to the history of the world, to give the Torah and the teachings of Judaism to the world.

That is why we are always counting: the Minyan, the days of the week and the Sabbath, the days between Pesach and Shavuot, which is coming in two days. Because these things are precious to us.

Every Jew is important, every congregation is important. It is a way of underlining how important is our purpose in life. How much we have to appreciate each other. How much we have to try to help each other. And to deserve our help from God. Amen.

Sermon 5 – Parashat Va'Etchanan – Deuteronomy 3:23-7:11 (July 1980)

Today's reading of the Torah contains the statement of the Shema: "Hear O Israel, the Lord Our God, the Lord is One". This is recognized as the fundamental statement of the Jewish faith: The Unity of God. The Torah reading also contains the Ten Commandments.

The Shema is in our prayer services, whereas the Ten Commandments are not. The Shema is the confession of faith at the time of one's death, known in Hebrew as Viddui. But the Shema also has a most interesting history.

The words that follow the verses comprising the Shema include, "And these words which I command you today should be on your hearts ... when you lay down in the evening to sleep and when you rise up in the morning."

The Shema was perhaps the oldest form of regular worship in the history of Judaism, to recite the words of the Shema morning and evening. And the reciting of the Shema became the occasion also for Jews to add prayers for help from God, known to us by the Hebrew word Tefillah. And this became the basic form of the fixed regular prayers: The reading of the Shema and the Tefillah.

It appears also that in very early times, the Ten Commandments were also added to the Shema, and they were recited together. This is evidenced by the Nash Papyrus, which dates from the time of the Hasmoneans, around the Second Century BCE.

But there arose groups within the Jewish community, including the early Christians, who began to teach that the Torah consisted only of moral teaching, and the teaching of the Unity of God. In other words, the Shema and the Ten Commandments were the only parts of the Torah that were really Divine. And so, the rabbis decreed that the reading of the Shema, which was enjoined in the Torah, should continue, with blessings, as we have it now. But the Ten Commandments should be omitted.

And to this day, we do not recite the Ten Commandments anywhere in our services. This is done to assert in the strongest terms that the entire Torah is holy, and that we as Jews remain faithful to the Mitzvot (commandments) which are contained in the Torah.

Thus, the Shema remained as the cornerstone of our prayer services, and the most fundamental statement of our faith. As an example, at the close of Yom Kippur, the last words that we say in the services of the day are the Shema, and the statement "God is the Lord".

And when a Jew wishes to signify, even when under great stress, and threat of death at the hands of enemies, that he is steadfast in the Jewish faith, he says the words of the Shema. And it can even be said in other languages, as long as the thought is expressed.

The rabbis were ready to change the order of our services, and drop the Ten Commandments, when it appeared that keeping it would fall into the dangers of isolating it and neglecting the rest of the Torah.

Now, when we recite the Shema in our services, we indicate both great principles. We assert the Unity of God, which we say with our eyes covered in order to concentrate on the meaning of the words, and we assert our adherence to the Torah as a body of Mitzvot and our joining with all other Jews in a statement of what unifies us all.

Sermon 6 – First Day of the Passover Holiday (April 1981)

The Seder and the questions of the four sons. They represent the youth, the progressive people, the people who have achieved all of the answers. Now, they ask the four questions.

The Evil Son asks: "What is this ceremony to you?" Usually, we take this to mean, "What is the meaning of this ceremony to you?" But the Talmud takes it to mean, "What good is it to you?" In other words, "What do you get out of it?" The implication is that the ceremony is useless.

We get this kind of question nowadays very often, "What's the good of observing Jewish practices?" The unspoken question is "What's in it for me?"

We have always had people who were only interested in what they could get immediately out of something or someone, for their own material gain. But we now live in an age that is especially notorious for its being a ME generation. There is a growing literature on the subject of how to see the whole world as a collection of people to be manipulated for one's own profit. For money and for power.

It is the classic example of what the late Martin Buber described as the I-It relationship, with the additional quality that the desired goal is purely material gratification and power.

Our answer as Jews is that we cannot accept such a point of view. For it means that everyone is for himself to the exclusion of the rest of the world, and if he were in Egypt he would not have been redeemed, because he would not have associated himself with the troubles of his generation.

We must strive very hard to avoid falling into the way of thinking "What's in it for me?". For our families, for our communities, for our synagogues, and for our fellow Jews in Israel, in Russia and in the Arab countries.

And, strange to say, when we put aside "What's in it for me?", we do get something very important. It is the satisfaction of having contributed to the betterment of the world, and to the increasing of peace in the world and in individual lives.

And even in a material sense, we benefit. For it provides a better world for us to live in. It gives us communities, and synagogues, which will be there when we suddenly feel the need for them. That there will be a land of Israel, when any Jew suddenly needs it. We will share in the saving of our people, in the Geulah.

Sermon 7 – First Day of the Sukkot Holiday (October 1981)

On the holiday of Sukkot there is the symbolism of the Four Species, known in Hebrew as the "Arba Minim". The Lulav (palm branch), the Etrog (citron), the Hadassim (myrtle leaves on three branches), and the Aravot (willow leaves on two branches).

There are many interpretations of the four species. One interpretation is that each species represents a different part of the human body.

The Lulav represents the spine, the spinal cord, and the leaves are like the ribs. Straight, strong, and proud.

The Etrog is shaped like a heart, which represents the mind and knowledge, our feelings, and our emotional attachment to our religion.

The Hadassim leaves are shaped like a human eye, to show that what we see must be evaluated in accordance with our religion. Also, to know that there is an eye (God) that is watching us.

The Willow is shaped like our lips and mouths, to know that what we say is very important, that the power of speech is what distinguishes us from the animals, and that we can cause great hurt and grief by improper use of this power. On the other hand, we can use it to instruct our youth, to convey our love and concern with our people, to express our thanks to God, and to say our prayers.

We take these four "kinds" together, tie them together, and hold them together when we make the blessing, to show that we are "integrated" personalities, that every part of us, and every aspect of our life, is working together for the common purpose. And that all Jews are together for the common purpose of the achievement of all that is good for the Jewish community, and for the world.

Chapter 10

Other Activities

The Eternal Light TV Show

My father served for a number of years as an adviser for the NBC television show called *The Eternal Light*. While my father was preparing his doctoral thesis in Oxford, *The Eternal Light* did an episode about Solomon Schechter in England at Cambridge University. My father mentioned in that episode that in Oxford they refer to Cambridge as the "other place".

Camp Tel Noar Weekends

I remember fondly going with my father to one of the Laymen's Institute weekends at Camp Tel Noar in New Hampshire where he was the guest speaker. It must have been in the early 1970's, but I can't remember the exact year. I do remember one thing that happened at the weekend. One of the "campers" was starting to tell a crude joke in our presence, and another "camper" told him to not say the joke out of respect for "The rabbi" (my father). It was one of those experiences where I realized that people don't speak to a rabbi the same way that they would speak to each other, out of respect.

I remember him talking about primitive man, and how ancient people didn't understand how the physical world works in the way that we understand it now. But those people weren't stupid. They just didn't know as much about the physical universe as we do now.

Visiting Professor

In the year 1973 my father served as a visiting professor at Brandeis University. My mother told me that he would travel up to the Boston area every week and would come back home for the weekend. During that time, I needed some minor surgery, and she told me that on one of the return trips from Boston my father hurried back to come visit me in the hospital during my recovery. I don't remember that visit, but it makes me feel good knowing that my father cared so much about me that he made sure to come visit me in the hospital.

At the time, my father was considering possibly making a career change and teaching full-time at Brandeis. But my understanding is that it would have been too much of an upheaval of our family for us all to move to Massachusetts. So, he didn't make that career move.

Lectures

I always thought that the main things that my father did were

Other Activities

teaching, writing Gittin, writing a few articles, and serving once in a while as a congregational rabbi or a High Holiday rabbi. But while going through his papers in preparation for writing this book, I discovered that he was also a prolific lecturer and gave many lectures in many locations across the United States, and some in Canada.

Chapter 11

Thoughts on Jews and Judaism

Self-Control

My father used to say that Judaism is essentially a religion of self-control. Judaism does not say that people must be denied the pleasures of life, but it does say that people should control and manage them. Judaism encourages its clergy to get married and have children. The Torah, in the Book of Numbers, Chapter 6, describes the Nazir, a person who takes it upon themselves to drink no wine or liquor. But Judaism frowns on those people who decide to become a Nazir, because doing so denies completely the enjoyment of life that God has created. In fact, after a Nazir's time period of self-abstinence is over, one of the sacrificial offerings that person is supposed to bring is a "sin offering", to atone for the sin of being a Nazir. The simple message is, "Enjoy life, but do so with some restraint".

Organic Judaism

My father used to say that one of the most important elements of living a Jewish life is the family. He used to explain that the family is an "organic" unit. The word organic as used in this context has nothing to do with how vegetables are grown without pesticides. The word "organ" means something that has a specific function within a larger "organism". Another way of saying it is that any organism is constructed from a collection of organs that function in a mutually helpful way. Each organ has its own role within the organism, and they all function harmoniously to achieve the organism's purpose.

As it relates to the Jewish family, each person has a role to play. There are concepts of mother and father, brothers and sisters, aunts and uncles, grandparents and grandchildren. And there are the resulting relationships that develop between each of those members of the extended family. My father felt very strongly that the future survival of the Jewish family depended on maintaining these traditional roles and relationships.

Charity

My father used to say that one of the most important things to keep in mind when donating money to charity is to make sure that you don't give away so much of your money that you end up making yourself poor and dependent on other people's charity.

We Chassidim

My father's father, whom I called my Zaida, came originally from the Ukrainian town of Mezhiritch. Another person that my father used to mention that was also from Mezhiritch was Judah David Eisenstein (JDE). JDE wrote several books, but the one that I remember my father mentioning specifically to me was the *Otzar Dinim Uminhagim*, which is a collection of laws and customs. He used to say that it was a very important work, especially because of its emphasis on tradition.

My father explained that the correct way to pronounce the name of the town is to put the accent on the second syllable, "zhi", and the consonant "zh" in that syllable should be pronounced like the zh sound in Russian or Ukrainian. That is how people who lived in that town pronounced the name of their own town. Many people in the United States mispronounce the name by putting the accent on the first syllable, and pronouncing the "zh" consonant just like the regular "z" consonant in English.

There were actually two towns called Mezhiritch. One was larger than the other, and the larger one was called Mezhiritch Gadol, or "Large Mezhiritch". The other one was called Mezhiritch Kattan, or "Small Mezhiritch". My paternal grandfather lived in Mezhiritch Gadol. This was also the town where the famous Chassidic Rabbi Dov Ber, known as the Maggid of Mezhiritch, lived. A Maggid is a preacher who delivers messages of wisdom. His Hebrew name was "Dov Ber", which itself is an interesting name because the word Dov in Hebrew means a Bear, and Ber in German also means a bear. There are a number of other common Jewish names that are formed in a similar way, by combining two words from different languages that mean the same thing. For example, the name "Menachem Mendel", which means Comforter in both Hebrew and Yiddish.

It is important to understand what the word Chassid means, and who are the people known as the Chassidim. The word exists in the Hebrew Bible, Deuteronomy 33:8, and means Loyal or Devoted. Thus, the Chassidim (the plural of Chassid) in the ancient days of Judaism were the people who were extremely devoted to God, regardless of the circumstances. Over time, the word has gained additional shades of meaning, including referring to the Chassidic movement that started in Ukraine in the 18th century.

Since my father's father came from the same town as the Maggid of Mezhiritch, the Gershfields considered themselves to be Chassidim. There are certain customs that developed among the modern Chassidim, which differ from traditional Judaism. My father used to say that "we Chassidim" don't ever say the weekday Tachanun prayers, which are a solemn and somber collection of prayers, because of the fact that every day of the year marks the death of at least one of the Chassidic rabbis. Note, I said the death, and not the birth, as you might think. These dates are considered "Hillula" days, or special celebrations. Hillula is an Aramaic word appearing in the Talmud (Shabbat 29b), which means "day of joy". So, to the Chassidim, every day of the year is a special day of celebration, because we want to celebrate the life and piety of those Chassidic rabbis, and therefore Tachanun is not said on any day of the year.

I remember hearing my father give a lecture in which he explained the difference between the Litvaks, that is the rabbis who lived and studied in Luthuania, and the Chassidic rabbis when it came to understanding certain Talmudic stories. One example that he gave was the description of Rabbi Yonatan Ben Uzziel who would study the oral law so fervently that the heat generated from his head would rise up in the sky and cook any bird in mid-flight as it flew over his head (Sukkah 28a). The Litvaks would study and analyze this paragraph in the Talmud by saying "I wonder whether or not it was a Kosher bird. And if a bird is flying and heat rises and causes it to be cooked in mid-air, is it permitted to eat the bird?" One the other hand, the Chassidim would say "Oy, What a learning! It was so strong that it could cook a bird in mid-flight!".

My father enjoyed telling the story of how one day the Gaon of Vilna, who was a through and through Litvak, decided to take a trip to visit the Baal Shem Tov, one of the greatest of the Chassidic rabbis (or perhaps it was to visit Dov Ber the Maggid of Mezhiritch - I don't remember precisely). As the story goes, when the Vilna Gaon entered the study room of the Baal Shem Tov, and the Baal Shem Tov realized who it was that was visiting him, the Baal Shem Tov shouted to the people standing in the room, "Throw the Litvak out!". The Vilna Gaon was taken aback, and he challenged the strong statement of the Baal Shem Tov, and said "What do you mean by wanting to throw me out? I came to visit you." Then, the Baal Shem Tov said, "No, no, you misunderstood me. I meant that you should throw out the Litvak that is inside of you".

Among Ashkenazic Jews, the strap of the Tefillin that is worn on the arm can be wrapped two different ways. One way is to wrap the strap in a clockwise direction, which is the Chassidic way, and the other way is to wrap it in a counterclockwise direction. My father's Tefillin were wound in the Chassidic way (clockwise around the arm), and because of that I wrap my Tefillin on my arm the same way.

Chesed Shel Emet

My father used to say that in Judaism attending a person's funeral is considered a "Chesed Shel Emet", or "A true kindness". Why is it called that? Because the person who is honoring someone else who has passed away is not expecting to get any reward in return from the deceased in exchange for the action. It is being done purely to honor the person who passed away. In some sense, my writing this book might be considered a Chesed Shel Emet, because I am writing it to honor my late father's memory, but as far as I know he is not able to repay me in any way.

The Yirei Hashem

There are several places in the Jewish scriptures were the Hebrew term "Yirei Hashem" is used. Literally, it mean "Those who revere the Lord". One prominent place is in Psalms 115, where this term appears twice (verses 11 and 13), and is included in the Hallel prayer. My father used to explain that it's not entirely clear to whom this term refers, however it probably does not refer to regular Jews. There are a number of different opinions of the major Jewish commentators regarding who those people really were. Some of those commentators include Rashi, Radak, Malbim and Ibn Ezra, among others. Ibn Ezra, for example, suggests that the term refers to righteous gentiles.

The Hebrew Word Makom

There are several Hebrew words that Jews use to refer to God. One of them is "HaMakom", meaning literally "The Place". The Hebrew word Makom appears in the Hebrew Bible a number of times, and is generally translated as "place" in English. Over time it became synonymous with God, and is used in traditional Jewish literature to refer to God. My father used to explain that its association with God comes from its appearance in the Book of Esther 4:14, where it says that "help will come from another place".

The Written Law and the Oral Law

My father once told me the story from the Talmud about the person who comes to Hillel and asks him to teach him the Torah, but only the written law and not the oral law. According to the story preserved in the Talmud in Tractate Shabbat 31a, Hillel agrees, but proceeds to teach the person in a way that proves that it is not possible to only learn the written law without also learning the oral law. I found Hillel's argument to be so compelling, and applicable to any sort of study of any text, that I feel it is worth repeating here.

Hillel starts teaching the Hebrew alphabet to the person. The next day, the person comes back for more training and Hillel reviews the letters that he had taught the day before, but this time he reverses the order of the letters and calls them by the "wrong" names. The person objects and points out that the day before Hillel called each of the letters by different names. Hillel then points out that the person's knowledge of what each letter is called depends entirely on what Hillel has told him. This shows that it is not possible to read any text without knowing something about the letters, the words, and their meanings, which can only be transmitted to the student orally. The point is that no matter how much information is written down about any subject, there needs to be some information that is transmitted orally so that the reader of the text can understand what the text means.

Two Types of Transgressions

My father would frequently say that in Judaism there are two main types of transgressions: Chayt and Avone. The Hebrew word Chayt, which comes from a verb using in archery meaning "to miss the mark", refers to making a mistake and doing the wrong thing. The Hebrew word Avone, on the other hand, refers to being rebellious against God, not just making a mistake. For example, denying God's existence or believing that the world wasn't created by God but rather by some random, totally meaningless, event. The first is more practical, and the second is more fundamental.

Large Steps

There is an important concept in Judaism regarding the observance of Shabbat. It is called "P'siot Gasot", and it means "Large Steps". This refers to the way that people walk. One's stride should not be large, the way that it is on regular weekdays when we are rushing about trying to get where we are going in a big hurry. On Shabbat, one should avoid P'siot Gassot because it is a reminder of how we behave during the work week. The Shabbat is supposed to be a day of rest, and we should not be rushing around the way we do on the other days of the week.

The Importance of the Aggadeta in the Talmud

My father used to explain that the Talmud contains two main types of material. There is the legal material, known as Halachah, that consists of statements of laws and their interpretations, and there is everything else. The Aramaic term that is used to refer to the "everything else" material is "Aggadeta". In fact, Aggadeta is a mixture of stories, parables, ideas, thoughts, and sayings. My father used to say that many people who study the Talmud like to skip over the Aggadeta portions, and just focus on the legal discussions. He felt that those people were doing an injustice to the Aggadeta, and that it is very important to study both the

Halachic as well as the Aggadic parts of the Talmud.

To help better understand what Aggadeta is, my father made the following analogy. Think about the various pieces of legislation enacted by the Congress of the United States. If you read the legislation, it tells you what the law is. But it doesn't tell you anything about the discussions that were going on at the time relating to that legislation, or discussions that people were having about other things in the society at that time. If you could gather together all of the newspaper and magazine articles that were published around the time that the legislation was enacted, and if you could read a log of all of the discussions that were held by members of Congress prior to the enactment of the legislation, you would be able to understand better why the legislation was needed and what it meant to people at that time. The Aggadeta in the Talmud serves that same purpose. It gives you the background of what was happening in society at the time of the Mishnah and Gemara, so that you can better understand the thought processes of the rabbis whose opinions are expressed in the Gemara.

On Prayers and Praying

When one says a Berakhah (the Hebrew word for "blessing"), it should be said slowly enough so that other people who are listening will be able to clearly hear and understand, so that they can honestly say Amen, which is a term of agreement. Many times I would say a Berakhah very quickly and my father would tell me to say it again more slowly and clearly. If one says the blessing too quickly, and people can't really hear the blessing clearly, then their "Amen" is not completely true, since they are merely assuming that one said the blessing correctly.

Rabbi Scholar Father Friend

My father would tell the story in the Talmud of a person who hears that a house in the town where he lives is on fire. The person should not pray to God that his own house is not the one on fire, since that would be equal to a prayer that asks God to change the outcome of some event. Whether or not that person's house is on fire is only a matter of finding out what happened and should not involve making any kind of prayer. This idea is contained in the Mishnah in Tractate Berakhot on page 54a.

My father used to say that you should not just thank God for the "good things" that you experience in your life. You should also thank God for the things that don't seem to be so good, since they are all part of God's plan. This idea is also contained in the same Mishnah in Tractate Berakhot on page 54a.

He used to say that when you wash your hands ritually before eating a meal with bread, you should first wash (actually, you just rinse) your hands, and then when you are drying your hands you should say the blessing "Al Netilat Yadayim". It's a little contrary to what you might think (since the blessing means "on washing the hands" and not "on drying the hands"), but that is the proper way to do it. Also, when you wash your hands ritually, you should make sure to pour water completely over your hands, not just the fingers or fingertips.

My father used to say that the Ashrei prayer begins the Minchah, or afternoon, prayer service because of its calming nature. It helps "set the mood" for the rest of the service. During the weekdays, we are usually busy either with our work or with our studies, and taking a break from those activities in order to attend a prayer service can be a difficult transition. The Ashrei prayer helps us to put aside the pressing needs and thoughts of the day, in order to be able to pray to God with the proper frame of mind.

Holiness

My father used to say that "holiness" in Judaism is based on the concept of "separation". The things that are "holy" are the things that are set aside as something special. For example, the Sabbath day is considered a holy day, because we treat it differently than the other days of the week. The area of the Temple was a holy place, because only certain people were allowed to enter. The tithes for the Kohanim that were taken from the grain that was grown in the fields were considered "holy" and were not allowed to be eaten by anyone else. Even the Land of Israel is called the "Holy Land" because it is something special and different than any other place on earth. And the Hebrew language is called the "Language of Holiness". My father wrote a chapter in a collection of essays in which he describes the way that the rabbi known as the Chatam Sofer viewed the holiness of the Torah.

The Definition of Sin

My father used to explain that the concept of sin among Jews is fundamentally different than the concept of sin among Christians. Jews believe that all people are born totally innocent of any sin. Whereas Christians believe that people are born with sin already inside of them, and that to rid themselves of the sin they need to believe in Jesus.

But this begs the question, What is sin? The Jewish definition of sin is rebellion against God's will. In other words, we Jews believe that God wants us to live a certain way, and to obey His commandments. And if we don't want to live the way that God wants us to live, and we disobey His commandments, then we are essentially rebelling against God. So, in Judaism, sinning isn't just doing something bad or morally wrong. It involves doing things that we know God does not want us to do, and we do them anyway in spite of knowing that God will probably end up punishing us for our disobedience.

The Jewish way of relieving us of our sins is to recognize that we have rebelled against God, and to commit to changing our ways and following His commandments, as well as asking God for His forgiveness.

What You Can't See

My father used to like to quote the Gemara in Tractate Berakhot 6a that said that there are lots of "Shaydim" (plural of the Hebrew word "Shayd", which means an evil spirit) floating around in the air, but you can't see them. And if you could see them, you would be terrified. According to that Gemara, if you want to actually see them you should create a certain concoction of various animal parts and turn it into a powder, and then put the powder into your eyes, and then you will be able to see the Shedim. My father used to add that if you put that powder into your eyes, then you will see all sorts of strange things (caused by putting toxic powder into your eyes – Disclaimer: Do NOT try doing this), not just the Shaydim. He used to have a pun involving the English word "shed" – if you hear strange noises from your back yard, it could be that there is a "shayd" in your shed.

Clean Language

My father used to mention the rabbinical concept of "Lashon

Nekiyah", or "clean language". This concept is mentioned in the Talmud, and means refraining from using negative sounding words even when talking about something that is negative. Instead, a negation of a good word indicates what we mean. For example, instead of saying that an idea is "bad", one would say it's "not good", thus avoiding the use of the word "bad". The idea of Lashon Nekiyah is different from the idea of a "euphemism", which is a nice word that refers to something that is not so nice. An example that my father used to give of a euphemism is the name of the Christian holiday Good Friday. That holiday should have been called Bad Friday because of what it commemorates, but instead it is called Good Friday as a euphemism.

People and Benefits

One of the important principles in Jewish law that my father used to mention is the idea that we assume that people want things that are to their benefit. Thus, in general we allow someone to receive a benefit without actually saying that they want it. This same principle exists in the common law of the United States. For example, banks will normally accept the deposit of a check into someone's account even if they didn't personally endorse the check, assuming that the check is made out in their name, because the assumption is that people normally would be happy to receive the money.

The same principle applies in the case of Jewish divorce. If the husband wants to give his wife a Get, and the wife cannot be located, we can make arrangements for someone else to receive and accept the Get on her behalf, since it is only to her benefit to do so.

Don't Change Too Much

One of the important ideas that my father used to say about Judaism is that if you try to make too many changes, or make too great a change in any particular area of Judaism, then it will cease to be Judaism and it will turn into something else. We need to be careful to maintain Judaism for what it is and has been, and to avoid making the kinds of fundamental changes that transform Judaism so much that it becomes no longer recognizable as Judaism.

One aspect of this idea is that sometimes the people who want to make changes to the religion have the best of intentions for themselves. For example, a woman might feel very strongly about wanting to put on Tefillin in the morning, which is traditionally only something that Jewish men have done. Their intentions for themselves are honorable and well-meaning. However, what can happen is that other people, whose intentions are not so well-meaning, can take those ideas for change and support them for other purposes. In our example of a woman who wants to put on Tefillin, other women may see that and then want to do so for the purpose of pure egalitarianism, basing their reasoning on the desire for complete equality of men and women in all aspects of the religion. Thus, people will start demanding changes to the religion for reasons that have nothing to do with the religion itself. When it comes to religion, changes need to be made in a very careful and cautious manner to avoid causing irreversible damage to the religion.

Getting Back to Basics

My father used to say that a lot of people get caught up in all sorts of complicated philosophical thoughts and arguments about the Jewish religion, and they forget about the basics. There are certain fundamental beliefs in Judaism, and those beliefs should be reviewed regularly, and time should be spent thinking about them and reminding ourselves how important they are.

Some basic beliefs of the Jewish religion include:

- The belief in One God

- The belief that God created the world from nothing. Note that this concept of the creation of the world is in opposition to the belief of Aristotle that the material world always existed, and was not created by a "Creator". Jews believe that God created the world, and that the world didn't come about just because of some random bumping together of bits of matter.

- The belief that God existed before the creation of the world and will exist after the world no longer exists.

Proper Synagogue Behavior

My father used to say that when one is attending a service in the synagogue and an older person, or a person who has more knowledge and wisdom than oneself, walks by, one should stand up and shake their hand as a sign of respect. It is not polite to stay seated while shaking someone's hand who is older or wiser.

Another thing my father used to say was that you should not attend a synagogue for any significant length of time without becoming a member. If you like the synagogue and want to attend regularly, then you should help to cover the costs of operating the synagogue, and the proper way to do that is to become a member of the synagogue.

Shabbat

My father used to explain what the basic idea of the Shabbat is, and how that concept relates to the various restrictions that observant Jews have on the things they can do on the Shabbat. Many people think of Shabbat as a "day of rest", implying that one shouldn't work on Saturdays because then one wouldn't be "resting". It's true that one aspect of Shabbat is the idea of not working. But another, and perhaps more fundamental, aspect of Shabbat is the idea of not creating new things. Jews believe that God created the world, and then stopped creating it. The world we live in is the result of God's creativity. The Shabbat is a time when we recognize God's completing the creation of our world by setting aside time every week when we don't engage in creative activities. For example, cooking food is not permitted on Shabbat because it results in the creation of a new state of the food. That is, food that is cooked has gone through a transformation from an "uncooked" state to a "cooked" state. Merely heating up food that has already been cooked is permitted on Shabbat, since it is not creating a new state for the food.

Call a Rabbi a Rabbi

My father used to say that when you address a rabbi either in conversation or in writing, you should always use the term rabbi together with their last name as a sign of respect. I always followed his rule, and even today it is hard for me to address a rabbi without using the term rabbi before their name, even if they say that it's OK to just refer to them using just their first name.

Thoughts on Jews and Judaism

Goring Oxen

There is a discussion in the Talmud about who is responsible for a goring ox. A lot of people would study this question and focus on the answers given as far as who the responsible party is for any damages that occur. My father looked at it another way. Before considering the answers of who is responsible, the question that my father raised was, "What is special about a goring ox and why are there specific laws pertaining to them?" The answer that he gave is that an ox is a castrated bull, which is normally much tamer than a regular bull. And that also means that it is very unusual for an ox to gore anyone or anything. So, if a person owns an ox and the ox starts goring people, at some point the owner will be liable for damages because it becomes clear that the particular ox is not as docile as an ox normally is, and the owner needs to protect people from the goring ox. A bull is assumed to be aggressive by its very nature, and therefore there is no question about when the owner of a bull is responsible for any damages that the bull causes. This is a great example of taking a step back when considering the discussions in the Talmud, and asking "Why is there a question in the first place?"

Sound and Silence

My father used to say that there was a period of a few hundred years in Jewish history that appears to be a "silent" period. That is, we don't have any record of any writings, thoughts, sayings or quotes from any Jewish leaders or thinkers who lived during those years. That time period extends from the end of the Prophets (around 500 BCE) to the beginning of the time of the Mishnah (around 100 BCE). Nobody has been able to explain adequately why this happened, and remains one of the great mysteries of

Jewish history. Once the time of the Mishnah began, Jewish scholars started to be quoted by name, and the silent period ended.

Another interesting point that my father used to make regarding sound and silence was that the first Jewish Temple in Jerusalem was a lively, noisy place with lots of music and singing. But the second Jewish Temple was much more subdued in its character, and a much quieter place.

Proper Burial Custom

My father told me that there is a Jewish custom when burying family members next to each other in a cemetery. You are not supposed to bury a male body with female bodies on both sides. So, for example, if a family plot has space for four bodies (for a father, mother, son and daughter-in-law), the two female bodies should be buried in the middle and the two male bodies should be buried on the outside. The issue here is that it isn't considered proper for a male to be surrounded by two females, even after they are dead and buried.

Hillel's Prozbul

My father used to explain that the greatness of Hillel and his Prozbul was that Hillel tried as much as possible to innovate within the existing Hallachic framework. Thus, the Prozbul is a document that addressed a real problem in the Jewish agricultural communities of ancient land of Israel, and it provides a practical solution to the problem that does not violate any existing Halachot.

Reading the Torah in the Synagogue

During the Shabbat morning service, and on Monday and Thursday mornings, the Torah is read from a Torah scroll. If a mistake is made during the reading, the reader needs to repeat the word or words that were read incorrectly and read them correctly. My father used to say that a lot of people do not follow the rules properly.

First, the main thing that needs to be done correctly is the pronunciation of the words themselves. That means that all the consonants and vowels need to be spoken correctly. If a mistake is made in the pronunciation of a word, or if a word is skipped completely by accident, the word needs to be said correctly. However, there is an exception to this rule, and the exception is that if the mistake in pronunciation does not materially affect the meaning of the word, then the word should not be repeated. A lot of people simply repeat the word using the correct pronunciation even if the incorrect pronunciation did not change the meaning of the word, but this is wrong and shouldn't be done.

Second, the musical notes, called tropes, that are used when reading the Torah are not as important as the pronunciation of the words themselves. So, if the reader said a word correctly, but used the wrong trope when reading the word, the reader should not go back and say the word again using the correct trope. Instead, the reader should just continue reading. My father used to say that a lot of people make this mistake of repeating words over again just because the trope was incorrect. The problem with doing this is that there is a rule that you should not repeat words in the Torah when reading them, since that would result in a text that is different than the text that is in the Torah.

Another thing that my father used to mention about reading the Torah in the synagogue is that a lot of people take the "yad", which is a pointer usually made of wood or metal with the tip shaped like a human hand (the Hebrew word "Yad" means "hand"), and rub the tip of the yad across the letters of the words that are being read. The problem with doing this is that the rubbing can cause the ink of the letters to flake off from the parchment that they are written on, and that would cause the entire Torah scroll to become unfit for use in the synagogue until it is repaired. Instead, the reader should just hover the tip of the Yad over the letters of the words as they are read, so that no rubbing occurs.

The Difference Between Hillel and Shammai on Lighting Channukah Candles

My father would try to understand the underlying reasoning behind various differences of opinion in the Talmud, rather than just taking them at face value. In other words, he was interested in knowing what the fundamental difference between the rabbis was when they are quoted as having different positions on a particular Halachic question.

As an example, my father used to explain what he thought was the underlying reason for the difference between Hillel and Shammai regarding the lighting of the Channukah candles. Before explaining the reasoning, let me describe the two approaches to lighting the candles.

On the holiday of Chanukah, which lasts for eight days, we light a different number of candles on each night of the holiday. According to Hillel, we light one candle on the first night, two candles on the second night, and so on, and we light eight candles on the eighth night. According to Shammai, we light eight candles on the first night, seven candles on the second night, and so on, and we light one candle on the eighth night. Basically, the number of candles increases each night according to Hillel and it decreases each night according to Shammai.

My father explained that the reason for the difference in opinion was based on a different understanding of what the actual miracle of Chanukah was.

Hillel believed that the miracle occurred as follows: A single jug of pure oil was found that should have lasted for only one day. But as the days went on, it kept burning day after day, and it wasn't clear how many days it could keep burning. Therefore, we start with one candle, to represent the first day, and on each subsequent day we add a candle to represent the number of days that the miracle continued until more pure oil could be produced.

Shammai, on the other hand, believed that the miracle occurred as follows: On the first day exactly one-eighth of the oil was consumed, and on the second day only exactly another one-eighth of the oil was consumed. This implied that after a total of eight days all of the oil would be consumed. Therefore, Shammai believed that the candles represented counting down to the last day, rather than a counting upward.

My own thought that I would like to add, if I may be so bold, is that these two approaches to the lighting of the Chanukah candles can also be applied to how we approach the days and years of our lives. We can approach them as counting down the amount of time we have left in our lives, since we know that our lifetimes are limited. In my mind, this is a pessimistic view of life, and it is sort of a countdown to the end. Or, we can approach them as counting up, meaning that we are always striving for doing more, learning more, improving our skills, and improving how we treat other people, without thinking that we are approaching a "finish line".

On Prayer

My father used to say that the proper way to lead the Psukei D'zimrah part of the morning service, part of which contains a series of Psalms that start and end with the word "Halleluyah", is to say the end of each Psalm and continue immediately to the word Halleluyah at the beginning of the next Psalm. This way, there is no separation between Psalms, and they flow one into the other as though they were all one giant Psalm.

The Aleinu prayer has gone through some changes in its history. One of the changes was the removal of a whole sentence near the beginning of the prayer. The word that begins the sentence immediately after the removed sentence has the letter Vav at the beginning. Normally the letter Vav has the meaning "and", however it sometimes means "but". In this context the meaning is "but". Without the deleted sentence, the Vav does not make sense. If you add the deleted sentence back into the prayer, then the Vav makes sense, as follows: "But we bow down and thank the King of the Kings of Kings, the Holy One, Blessed be He".

My father used to say that the Hebrew phrase "Melech Malchei Ha'mlachim", which appears in the Aleinu prayer, needs a little explanation. It means "The King of the Kings of Kings". This seems like a strange way to refer to God. The explanation is that this phrase was intended to mean that although there have been some religious leaders in history who called themselves the King of Kings, Judaism considers God to be greater than all those leaders. In that sense, God is the King of all those Kings of Kings.

The phrase "Boruch Hu U'Varuch Sh'mo" should only be said in the middle of a Brachah (as a response to the initial "Boruch Ato Adoshem" part of the Brachah when someone else is reciting the Brachah) if the person who is hearing the Brachah is not fulfilling any obligation. For example, if you are listening to the repetition of the Amidah prayer, and the leader of the service says the "Boruch Ato Adoshem" at the end of the first prayer, then you should say "Boruch Hu U'Varuch Sh'mo", since you have already fulfilled your obligation to say the Amidah prayer and you are just listening to the repetition of the prayer by the Sh'liach Tzibbur. If however, the leader of the service is doing a shortened version of the Amidah prayer, where the leader will not repeat the entire Amidah after everyone is done reciting it individually, then you should NOT say "Boruch Hu U'Varuch Sh'mo", since that would cause an interruption in your prayer which is not allowed. Essentially, the Sh'liach Tzibbur is reciting the prayer on your behalf, as opposed to just repeating it, so you need to be silent and just say Amen at the end of each Brachah.

In the Aleynu prayer, there is a verse that begins with "Va'Anachnu Kor'im …". The interesting thing is the letter Vav that is at the beginning of the word Va'Anachnu. Sometimes the letter Vav can mean "and", and other times the letter Vav can mean "but". In this case it means "but". However, if you read the Aleynu prayer from the beginning, you realize when you arrive at the beginning of that verse that it does not make sense to say "but" at that point. The explanation is that originally there was another verse just before that verse in the Aleynu prayer. The other missing verse said, "For they pray to a god who will not save them". Now, the meaning of "Va'Anachu Kor'im" makes sense. It mean "But we, on the other hand, bow, pray and give thanks to the King of the Kings of Kings, the Holy One Blessed be He."

On Praying

My father used to tell me that when you say Amen to someone's Brachah, you should not say it in a louder voice than the person saying the Brachah. The Amen serves as an acknowledgement of the words of the Brachah, and not as its own statement.

When saying the Shema prayer, one should take the Tzitzit and wind them around the little finger of one's left hand until reaching the last paragraph of the Shema. Then, one should take the Tzitzit in one's right hand and kiss them at the appropriate times. This allows one's right hand to be free to move around and turn the pages while the left hand holds the Tzitzit.

My father used to say that a common mistake that people make when saying the Hallel prayer, which is said on Holidays and Rosh Chodesh (the beginning of a new Jewish month), is to put the emphasis on the "li" syllable in the phrase "Hatzlichah Na". Instead, the correct syllable to emphasize is "chah".

On Whether to Decide Strictly

My father used to say that whenever there is a Halachic decision to be made in a specific case, it is always easy to take the strict approach and not permit something. The more difficult thing to do, and the thing that shows how much you really know about the

Halachah, is to find a way to be lenient and to permit something and still abide by the Halachah.

Family Customs

For the first half of his life, my father never grew a beard. But when his father passed away in the 1980's, he started growing a beard. Once the Shloshim (first 30 days after death of a close relative) period of mourning was over, he continued to grow his beard and he told me that the custom in his family was that men would not shave off their beard after their father passed away, as a sign of respect. I have done the same thing, and I have not shaved off my beard since my father passed away in 2019.

When a person loses their mother or father, they are supposed to tear one of the garments that they are wearing as a sign of mourning. When my father's father passed away, my father ripped his jacket lapel. He showed me years later that he had done that. Nowadays, some Jews will just tear a small piece of material and pin it onto their clothing. But my father did it the traditional way. When my father passed away, I tore shirt of mine that I liked. In my mind, it is more meaningful if you tear a piece of clothing that is valuable rather than just tearing a small piece of cloth that has very little value.

Tashlich Observance

One of the things that my father used to mention as an example of how people overdo things unnecessarily when they observe certain Jewish customs and traditions is the observance of the Tashlich custom. The Hebrew word Tashlich comes from the word that means "to throw", and there is a verse in Micah 7:19

that says that God will throw all of our sins into the water. So, the custom arose to throw something that represents our sins into a river during the afternoon of the first day of Rosh Hashanah (the Jewish New Year). Most people throw a small piece of food, like a piece of bread for example.

The problem is that some people take the custom to the extreme and throw very large amounts of food into a river or stream, like a whole loaf of bread. My father used to say that you only need to throw a few crumbs, not a whole loaf, or even a single slice of bread. There is a principle in Judaism called "Bal Tash'chit", which means that you should not destroy food. Throwing a whole bagel, for example, into a river would result in the destruction of edible food, which is not permitted according to Jewish law. The crumbs are just supposed to be symbolic of our sins that we want to cast away. When we throw the crumbs into the water, we aren't throwing our actual sins away. The number of pounds of food doesn't need to equal the number of our sins. And we aren't supposed to be throwing away a large amount of usable food because of the Bal Tash'chit principle of not destroying food.

On Jewish Leadership

My father used to say the following about two of the great leaders of the Jewish people mentioned in the Torah, Moses and Aaron. Each of these leaders, who happened to be brothers, had a certain flaw in their leadership.

In the case of Moses, the real reason why he was not allowed by God to enter the land of Israel was that he gave in to the demands of the people who wanted to send spies to the land to see how good it was and how easy it would be to conquer after entering the land. Instead of giving in, and allowing the spies to investigate, Moses should have told the people that God promised to give a land of milk and honey to the Jews, and that God's promise is enough. It would be an insult to God to go take a look and see for themselves instead of relying on their faith.

In the case of Aaron, the story of the Golden Calf similarly illustrates a lack of leadership because Aaron gave in to the people's demands to create an idol shaped like a cow. He should have tried to talk them out of it, and told them that Moses would be coming down from the mountain very soon and that they should have faith. Instead, he gave in to their demands. And afterwards, when Moses finally came down from the mountain, Aaron tried to make it sound like he wasn't responsible. My father would emphasize the exact words that the Torah records Aaron as saying, that the gold was put in the fire and "out popped a calf". As though nobody actually took the gold and shaped it into a calf. So, not only did Aaron shirk his responsibility as a leader, but he also tried to act as though he wasn't involved in the creation of the calf and that somehow it just created itself.

The takeaway from both of these leaders is that a great Jewish leader should not give in to the wishes of the people being led, if their wishes go against the wishes of God.

Which is Better, Memory or Analysis?

My father used to mention the debate in the Talmud regarding which is a better quality for a scholar to have, a great memory or great analytical ability? The Talmud appears to lean toward the answer that a great memory is more important. One example is the story that is told in Tractate Berakhot 64a about Rabba and Rav Yosef, who were candidates to become the head of a Yeshiva. Rabba had great analytical ability, while Rav Yosef had an amazing memory. A question was sent to the Jewish scholars in the Land of Israel, which is more important? The response that was received said that a great memory is more important, because it gives the person the material to use for their analysis.

What the Talmud is saying is that it is better to have a great memory, because if you can memorize a large quantity of material, then you will be able to think about all of that material and come to strong conclusions. If, on the other hand, you don't have a good memory, but you do have a great ability to analyze legal issues, then it will be harder for you to think about legal questions that arise, since you won't have the raw materials in your head with which to form conclusions. It is important to remember that at the time of the Talmud there were no computers or the Internet, and book printing and publishing had not yet been invented, so if you didn't have a good memory you were at a very large disadvantage compared to someone with a very good memory.

Study Quickly or In Depth?

One time I asked my father which way is better to study the Talmud: Is it better to study a lot of material without going into depth or is it better to study small amount of material and study them in great depth. He answered me by saying that both are important, and in fact in the great Yeshivot of Lithuania they would spend half of their time each day doing rapid reading and studying of texts, and the other half would be spent learning specific topics in depth. One of the popular study methods these days is to join the Daf Yomi or Mishnah Yomit (daily study of a page of Talmud or Mishnah), which does rapid study of the entire Talmud or Mishna texts one page per day. But I haven't heard that there is currently a popular study method of learning specific topics in depth along with rapid reading of a daily page. It would probably be better if people also studied certain topics in more depth than they are doing so with the Daf Yomi or Mishnah Yomit programs.

Modern Questions

One time my father visited a yeshiva and asked a question about a passage in the Mishnah that was not one of the traditional questions one asks as a student in the yeshiva. After the students tried unsuccessfully to loate my father's question in the list of questions they were studying, they finally turned to my father and said, "You must be from JTS".

Biblical Characters

Moses

My father used to say that many people think that the sin that Moses committed which resulted in him not entering the Land of Israel was his hitting the rock to produce water instead of speaking to the rock as God had instructed him. This is a convenient explanation, and it says as much in the verses of the Torah. But, according to my father, the real reason that Moses was not allowed to enter the land was because of the incident with the spies. The people wanted to send spies into the land to see what it was like before actually entering. They had an ulterior motive, which was to find fault with the land and to generate fear among the people.

The sin that Moses committed, and which was so great that he was not allowed to enter the Land of Israel because of it, was agreeing to send the spies into the land. He should not have agreed to send the spies, and instead he should have told them that they needed to have faith in God, and that God would help them to overcome any obstacles. Since Moses did not try to instill this faith in God into the minds and hearts of the people, he was punished.

Abraham

The story of the binding of Isaac seems to be a simple test of whether or not Abraham will obey whatever command God gives him regardless of the consequences. But my father went further and explained that God actually was testing Abraham's faith in God's promise to make from him a great nation. In order for God's promise to be fulfilled, Isaac needed to stay alive so that he could have children of his own and eventually his children's children would multiply into the great nation that God promised. The test was whether or not Abraham trusted God enough to follow his command to sacrifice his only son, even though that would conflict with the prior promise made by God to make a great nation from his descendants.

Joseph

According to my father, Joseph is one of the few people in Jewish history known as "So-and-so The Tzaddik", meaning "So-and-so The Righteous". It is because of Joseph's ability to resist temptation while living the house of Potifar, and having been left alone in the house with Potifar's wife, that he earned this title.

My father also used to say that most people focus on the relationship between Joseph and his brothers in the "Joseph story" in the Book of Genesis. However, according to my father, the more important relationship in the story is between Joseph and his father Jacob.

When Joseph reveals himself to his brothers in Egypt, the first thing he asks them is "Is my father still alive?" my father used to read this sentence as follows: "Is my father still alive, in spite of all of the horrible things you did to him and all of the stress that you caused him?"

David

My father used to tell about how King David was very remorseful for his sin regarding Bathsheba and her husband Uriah the Hittite, and it bothered him for the rest of his life. Even though he asked for forgiveness from God many times, he was never sure that he had been forgiven. According to the Midrash quoted in Tractate Sanhedrin 107b, God told King David that He would show that David was forgiven, but not during his lifetime. Rather, it would become clear during the lifetime of his son King Solomon. When Solomon built the Temple and it came time to bring the Ark into the Holy of Holies, the gates refused to open until King Solomon invoked the name of his father King David, as hinted at in Psalm 24, thus showing that King David had been forgiven.

A Third Beit HaMikdash

My father used to say that perhaps we shouldn't wish too hard for the Beit HaMikdash to be rebuilt, because if it were rebuilt he could imagine what it would look like: There would be hundreds, if not thousands, of vendors of all kinds near the Beit HaMikdash selling trinkets and many other kinds of silly items in order to make money from the people visiting the holy site, as though it was a tourist attraction. There would be jugglers and singers, comedians and freak shows. Instead, if it existed, the

Beit HaMikdash should be treated as a very holy and sanctified place and should not be trivialized into a money-making tourist attraction.

Using the English Word God in Print

My father used to say that the people who don't want to print the word God with all of the letters (G,o,d) in order to avoid writing down the name of God are misguided. If you read various English language books or articles that have been written about Jewish religious topics, many times you will come across spellings like this: G-d, Gd, G'd, G_d, etc. My father said that there is no need to go to those lengths, since the word God is not actually a name of God, and it isn't event written using the holy Hebrew letters.

The Prophet Ezekiel and Jews in Exile

My father used to say that the prophet Ezekiel had a profound influence on the lives of Jews living in exile. Ezekiel basically said that Judaism is not dependent on the existence of the Temple (Beit HaMikdash), or on living in the Land of Israel. Jews can create communities outside of the Land of Israel, and can continue to pray and study and lead Jewish lives while in the Galut. Prior to Ezekiel, there was a strong feeling that Jews needed to live in the land of Israel and could not properly function as Jews elsewhere.

On Being a Cantor

In the years 2001 and 2002, I served as a High Holiday Cantor in New Jersey. I remember my father telling me that if you are going to be a Cantor for the High Holidays, you should expect, and request, to be paid a reasonable fee for your work. There are some people who are willing to officiate as a Cantor for either very low pay, or no pay. His opinion was that this is not a good thing to do, since it will result in synagogues expecting Cantors to work for nothing. And this will make it hard for professional Cantors to make a living. In fact, this has happened at many synagogues, where the position of professional Cantor has been totally eliminated. Instead of hiring a Cantor, those synagogues rely on volunteers from the membership to lead services. This saves some money, but it is questionable whether those synagogues are better off than they would be with a full-time Cantor.

My father used to say that whenever you learn how to lead the services, you should first try to understand what the "basic Nusach" is for that part of the service. The Hebrew word Nusach refers to a traditional melody or set of short musical phrases that have been passed down through the generations. Each major service, or part of a service, has a particular Nusach associated with it. Then, once you have the basic Nusach clear in your mind, you can start making your own variations and embellishments. But whatever you do, you should always keep the music grounded in the basic Nusach.

It is also important to gain a basic understanding of music theory, at least to the point where you can distinguish major, minor, and Freigish keys, as well as how to transition from a minor key to its related major and the other way around.

Another thing that my father told me about being a Cantor. If you have served as the main High Holiday Cantor at a synagogue, and got paid for doing so, then you can legitimately call yourself a Cantor. It isn't necessary to have a degree from a Cantorial School. As long as a synagogue is willing to pay you to be their main High Holiday Cantor, that alone is enough to establish you as a professional Cantor.

Chapter 12

Words of Wisdom

My father used to say, jokingly, that he was always ready to give advice, known in Yiddish as "Ey-tzess", to people for no charge. This section includes as many of his free words of wisdom that I am able to include in this book.

Getting a Part-Time Job

One time, when I was in college at Columbia, I thought that it would be a good idea for me to earn some money to help pay the tuition. I looked around for a part-time job and found one listed in the Columbia Spectator for a newspaper delivery job. The requirements included getting up around 4 AM each day to deliver the newspaper around campus. The pay wasn't much, but at least it was something. I remember that when my father found out about my plan, he told me that it was more important to spend my time studying and learning, rather than getting up so early in the morning to deliver newspapers. And I would have gotten tired out and not been able to study well during the day. I followed his advice and I'm glad I did.

Life Advice

My father used to say that you should not keep wondering when you will become famous, as though you are looking over your shoulder to see whether fame is creeping up on you. If it happens, it happens. But don't keep hoping that you will become famous, and wondering when it's going to happen. This idea is expressed in the Book of Proverbs. My father used to tell a joke about this: There was a man who tried to achieve fame by following this advice. He tried very hard not to worry about whether or not he was going to become famous. But he wasn't becoming famous, and he complained to his rabbi. The rabbi told him that it was true that you should not worry about it, but that man's problem was that he kept looking over his shoulder to see when fame was about to catch up with him.

Don't be overly modest. If you keep telling people that you are no good at something, and that you don't know much about something, then eventually they will believe you. This will make it difficult for you to accomplish things, get a job and make a living.

My father used to say that if you want to be a real "Mentsch", you should always pay your bills on time. That is much more important than how many times a day you pray or put on Tefillin, whether you pray with a Minyan, or how much Torah study you engage in.

My father used to say that if you attend a synagogue regularly, then you should become a member, assuming that you can afford the membership fee. It is not proper to use the services of a synagogue and not support it financially. At a minimum, you should give a donation to the synagogue to help cover some of their expenses. If you are a student, and don't have any income or have very little income, that's understandable. But if you are working and have a salary, you should pay for a membership in any synagogue that you attend regularly.

My father frequently mentioned the concept that is described in the Talmud of not getting someone's hopes up falsely. For example, if a person knows for certain that they are not going to buy anything in a retail store, that person should not even go into the store because that will cause the storekeeper to think that they want to buy something, and that's not proper.

Another thing that my father used to mention, that is also in the Talmud, is that spouses should be honest with each other and not use psychological tricks like reverse psychology to get your spouse to do what you want. The relationship between a husband and wife is based on mutual trust, and if one behaves in such a way that one reduces the level of that trust in the marraige, then the marriage will suffer.

How to Think About Studying

My father used to say that there are two ways that you can approach the study of a Tractate of the Talmud. The first way is to start on the first page, and think to yourself "I can't believe how many more pages I need to learn in order to get through this giant Tractate". This approach is not good. The better approach is to think as follows: "Look at what I have accomplished so far! I have finished the first page, and now I can continue on to the second page, and eventually I will finish the entire Tractate."

This idea can be derived from the verse in Kohelet (Ecclesiastes) 10:2, which says "The heart of the wise man is at his right, whereas the heart of the fool is at his left."

Make Your Study Regular

My father used to say that Judaism requires us to make studying our religious texts a regular part of our lives. The important thing is that the study should be regular. The amount of material that you study is not as important as making it a regular habit. And the study doesn't need to be every day. It could be every other day, or even just one special day during the week that you set aside time to study. Done this way, the Torah - which literally means "instruction" - will have an impact on one's life.

Of course, your studying should be frequent enough that it feels like it is a normal part of your life. So, for example, if you only study once a month, or one a year, then that would not qualify as regular study.

There are a number of places in the Mishnah where this idea is mentioned. In the Mishnah of Masechet Peah, 1:1, it says "These are the things that have no specifically required measure: ... the study of Torah". The Mishnah is emphasizing that the exact amount of study is not the main thing when it comes to Torah study. In another place, Pirkei Avot 1:15, the Mishnah says "Shammai used to say: Make your Torah study regular". The word that the Mishnah uses is "Keva", which literally means "fixed". But my father used to explain that it means that your study should be "regular". It doesn't have to be at a "fixed" time of day, or on any fixed day of the week, rather it should be done on a regular basis, whatever fits into your own personal schedule.

Making a Living is Hard

My father used to like to quote the section in the Talmud, Tractate Pesachim 118a, that discusses the Great Hallel prayer. This prayer is essentially Psalm 136, and is recited on Shabbat mornings. Note that the numbering of the Pslams that we have today apparently did not exist in the time of the Talmud, as evidenced by the fact that the Talmud never refers to any Psalm by its number, rather by the opening words of the Psalm in Hebrew.

Rabbi Shaizvi is quoted as saying, in the name of Rabbi Elazar the son of Azarya, that Psalm 136 has two phrases that are related: The splitting of the Red Sea and the making of a living. Rabbi Shaizvi explained that the Psalm mentions both items because the difficulty of making a living is on the same level of difficulty as the splitting of the Red Sea. The message is, "Work hard at your career, and don't give up, because it won't be easy".

Learning Is Easier When You are Young

My father used to say that the human mind is able to absorb tremendous amounts of information, facts, ideas, and material when a person is young. It gets harder as one gets older. That is one reason why it is a good idea to try to get as much education as possible when you are in your elementary school years, teenage years and even in your 20's and 30's. In 1980, my father gave a speech to the graduating class of the Prozdor program for high school students at JTS in which he said essentially the same thing. He also made a reference to the Talmud, Tractate Shabbat 21b, where Abaye says that he regrets not learning something while he was young, since it didn't become part of his "youthful learning", or "Girsa D'Yankuta" in Aramaic.

Understanding Midrash

My father used to explain that there is a certain plan or structure to Midrashim, which is the plural of the Hebrew word Midrash. A midrash is usually translated in English as "exegesis", and usually refers to a rabbinical interpretation of a passage in the Jewish scriptures. I heard from one of his students that he would make an analogy between professional wrestling and Midrash. Both have a certain choreography, and they follow a predictable pattern: Preamble; Act One, Act 2, Act 3, The Moral. The idea that the midrash wants to convey has been determined already, and the midrash "plays out" the sequence of steps to get to the conclusion, just as a professional wrestling match has a start, several acts, and a conclusion with a message, all of which have been choreographed ahead of time.

Advice for Other Rabbis

My father used to get letters and phone calls from other rabbis asking him for his advice on how to handle various situations that arose within their congregations. Even though my father was not that experienced as a congregational rabbi, he had a very good sense of what should be done in different situations to help resolve disputes and reduce tension.

Difference Between Heaven and Hell

My father used to say, "What's the difference between the people who end up in Heaven versus those people who end up in Hell?" He would then say that in both Heaven and Hell when it comes time to eat a meal, all people in both places will have their arms tied together in front of them, meaning that each person is not able to bend their arms. In Hell, the people who are all seated next to each other at the dinner table only care about themselves, so they are not able to eat any of the food that is set out in front of them, and they suffer because of this. But, in Heaven, the people who are seated next to each other are not only interested in themselves, and so they all take some of their food and feed the people next to them, which does not require bending their arms. There is a famous story called the "Allegory of the Long Spoons", commonly attributed to Rabbi Haim of Romshishok, Lithuania, and this is probably what he was referring to. I think that the version of the story that my father used to tell, where people's arms are tied together, makes more sense because if you have a spoon with a handle which is longer than your arm you could just hold the spoon somewhere in the middle of the handle instead of all the way at the end of the handle, and get the food into your mouth even if your arms are bound together. However, if you just have regular cutlery, If your arms are bound together so that you can't bend them, and your arms are longer than the handles on the cutlery, then you won't be able to put food into your own mouth.

New York City Isn't Winnipeg

When my father was growing up in Canada, there was no rich class and there was no poor class. There were no slums. Some people had a little more money, and some people had a little less money. In New York City, on the other hand, there is a very wide range of amount of money that people have and that they spend. In the old days in New York City, it was illegal to do gambling, and places were raided. But only the poor places were raided. Petty gambling fulfills a desire on the part of the poor to break out of their poverty, and suddenly become wealthy. They can't get rich slowly, and the only way to get rich is quickly. Eventually, the state provided a product for this: The Lottery. All you have to do is buy a little ticket and perhaps you'll "get rich quick". In my father's opinion, it's a great illusion and dream that the state creates, but the people like it and want it, and that's why it's there.

Military Life

My father himself was never in the military, however his older brother Max joined the Canadian Air Force and his father-in-law served in the Canadian Army. An uncle of his was in the Russian Army. So, he had some interesting things to say about military life.

One thing he mentioned was that in the Canadian military you could have as much food to eat as you wanted at mealtimes, however you had to make sure to finish all of the food that you took. If you didn't finish eating all of it, you would be punished. This was intended to reduce waste.

Another thing my father used to say was how things get done in the field. Suppose some army vehicles are traveling along a road and come upon a tree that fell down and was blocking the road. How would the tree get moved out of the way? The commanding officer would tell the soldiers, "Move that tree!" and they would move the tree. The point of this story is to illustrate the concept of delegation.

Chapter 13

Stories

On the Subway

One day my father was riding the subway in Manhattan, and a man sitting next to him pulled out a very large kitchen knife from his bag and started playing with it in an ominous way. My father looked at the knife and said to the person holding it "What are you going to do with that, make a bologna sandwich?" To which the person responded, "Hey, you're OK!" Apparently, my father's statement calmed the person down enough so that he didn't feel the need to use the knife to attack anyone on the train.

Panhandlers in Midtown Manhattan

There were occasions when my father was walking through midtown Manhattan and people would approach him asking for a handout of money. My father would ask them what they wanted the money for. If they said that they were hungry and needed the money to buy food, he would tell them that he would gladly pay for them to buy a meal in one of the local restaurants. But they had to go into the restaurant and actually purchase a meal, which he would then pay for. Almost nobody ever took him up on his offer of assistance, probably because they didn't really want money in order to eat. They probably wanted the money for other purposes, and were just using that as a way of making people feel sorry for them.

Limousines

One time when I was interviewing for a job in the late 1970's, a stretch limousine came to pick me up from our apartment in Manhattan and take me to New Jersey for the interview. When my father saw the large black limousine, he told me that he usually has a negative reaction whenever he sees a limousine because it reminds him of the black hearses that would always be at a funeral. Apparently, he was not able to disassociate the image of a limousine from the idea of a funeral.

Heard on the City Bus

My father used to tell the true story about something that he saw and heard on a New York City bus one day. There was a somewhat overweight woman standing in front of a couple of young men who were seated. One of the men said to the other one in Hebrew, "Teyn laparah lashevet", which means "Let the cow sit." Unfortunately for them, the woman who was standing also knew Hebrew and said to the men in Hebrew, "Haparah yecholah la'amod", meaning "The cow is able to stand." When you live in New York City, you never know who is going to understand what you are saying in a foreign language, so you need to be careful what you say in public.

Now We are Just Jews

One time my father was riding the city bus with my mother, and a Jewish woman got on the bus. She sat down next to my father and started chatting. She mentioned that she was very annoyed with all of the Soviet Jews who were moving into the city, and how she just couldn't stand those "Eastern Jews" (OystYuden). My father responded, "After the Holocaust, there are no more Eastern Jews or Western Jews, there are just Jews".

Greenwich Village

One day, soon after moving to New York City, my parents decided to explore Greenwich Village. It just happened that there was an art festival going on at the time. There was an artist creating portraits of people, for a small fee, by etching a person's face onto a small rectangular piece of metal and then framing it. The portraits were all done such that the person's face was viewed from the side, sort of like a silhouette. My mother noticed that all of the samples that the artist had hanging on a display board had the people's faces looking to the left. She was thinking that it would be nice to have a pair of faces, hers and my father's, with one facing to the right and one facing to the left, so that when they would be hung on the wall it would look like the faces were looking at each other.

The artist said "no" to my mother's request. My mother was taken aback and asked why he couldn't fulfill her request. He answered that he only learned how to do this kind of portrait one way, and he was unable to draw people's faces looking in the opposite direction.

My Grandfather's Visit to Manhattan

Once, when my father's father was visiting him in Manhattan, my father tried to impress his father by showing him around downtown Manhattan. He showed him the big buildings – to which his father said (in Yiddish) "In Winnipeg Iz Dee Zelba Zach (it's the same thing in Winnipeg)". So, my father said, "Really, do they have such big buildings in Winnipeg?" His father said, "A building is a building, maybe a little bigger or a little smaller, but the idea is the same". Then my father showed him the George Washington Bridge, and how big it was. His father was not impressed: "We have bridges in Winnipeg also". Then something happened. It was around lunch time, and there was a hot dog stand on the sidewalk. A man came running out of one of the buildings and slammed down some cash on the stand and grabbed a hot dog in a bun and started running down the street eating it as he ran. My grandfather asked my father, "What's that?" My father answered, "That's someone eating his lunch". Then my grandfather said, "That we don't have in Winnipeg".

On the Air Quality in New York City

Once in a while, my father would travel from Manhattan to visit Camp Ramah in the Berkshires in Wingdale NY. After spending a few days there, upon his return to Manhattan he would feel funny. He finally realized that all of the fresh air in the camp was affecting him negatively. He used to say that his solution was to stand outside on the sidewalk behind a city bus and inhale the exhaust fumes for a few minutes, and this would make him feel better.

Don't Break a Leg

My father used to tell us as kids when running to catch the school bus on the sloping sidewalk when there is snow on the ground: "It is better to be late than to break your leg" – my father said that it was an "ancient saying" that he just made up. Two schoolteachers from Israel, who happened to be visiting JTS, heard my father telling us this "ancient saying". Being experts in the Hebrew language, they put it into a rhyming Hebrew phrase: "Tov L'Acher MeRegel L'Shaber". Meaning, literally, "It is better to be late than a leg to break".

Rabbi Eliezer Silver

Rabbi Silver was a well-known rabbi who had a driver who used to drive him wherever he needed to go. One time, Rabbi Silver's driver was speeding along the highway on a late Friday afternoon to get to the hotel in time for Shabbat. The car was pulled over by a police officer. The driver said to the officer: "Do you know who that person is in the back seat? It's the Chief Rabbi of the United States!". Hearing that, Rabbi Silver tapped his cane on the floor and said, "AND Canada".

The Police Horse and the Student

It was around the time of the protests at Columbia University in 1968. One of my father's students was complaining that while he was attending the riots at Columbia, a police horse had attacked him and injured him. My father proceeded to explain that he grew up in Winnipeg and, having lived in that area for many years, he was very familiar with horses. One thing he knew for certain was that a horse won't follow you up the stairs and into your bedroom to attack you. If the student had been in his room studying instead of outside watching the protests and riots, he would not have had the encounter with the police horse and would not have been injured.

On a related note, my father used to tell the story of his father visiting from Winnipeg during those disturbances at Columbia University. My father asked him, "Would you like to go see a riot? There's one scheduled for this afternoon at the Columbia University campus". His father agreed to go and take a look. At one point, the protesters started getting very loud and rowdy. My father's father tugged on his arm and said (in Yiddish) "Let's go". Apparently, the images of the students rioting on campus brought back memories of the pogroms in Europe that he had escaped by emigrating to Canada decades earlier.

Chapter 14

Humor

My father had a very good sense of humor, and he used it to great advantage when interacting with students, fellow faculty members and with audiences of his lectures and speeches. This section includes a variety of humorous stories and jokes that he used to tell. As my father used to say, "Enjoy, enjoy!"

A Litvak, which means a Lithuanian Jew, told a certain Chassid that the Chassid's rabbi isn't very great. So, the Chassid said, "Every Motzaei Shabbos Eliyahu Hanavi (Elijah the Prophet) comes and learns with my rabbi". The Litvak said, "That's not possible". The Chasid said, "It must be true because my rabbi told me himself". So, the Litvak said, "Then your rabbi is a liar". So, the Chassid said, "If my rabbi is a liar, then why would Eliyahu Hanavi come every Motzaei Shabbos and learn with him?"

Rabbi Scholar Father Friend

My father used to tell the following British joke, which depends on understanding the multiple puns in the joke. There were three drunks on a train in England. As the train was approaching a station, the first drunk asked the others, "Is this Wembley?" To which the second drunk replied, "No, it's Thursday". To which the third drunk replied, "I'm thirsty too, let's have a drink!"

A group of Jews who were Amaratzim (a Yiddish word that means uneducated and ignorant, a short form of the plural of the Hebrew words Am Ha'aretz) were in a certain synagogue and felt that they were being mistreated, not given Aliyot to the Torah, or given a good seat. So, they established their own synagogue called the "Bet HaKnesset Shel Amaratzim", which means "Synagogue of the Ignorant".

They created a bylaw that said that only Amaratzim are allowed to be members of the synagogue. One day, on the Shabbat of Parashat Korach, they called up the Kohen to the first Aliyah. The Torah reading starts with the Hebrew words "Vayikach Korach Ben Yitzhar ...", meaning "And Korach the son of Yitzhar took ..." - "Wait!", said the Kohen. "It looks like a word is not spelled correctly in the Sefer Torah that is being read today". It says "Korach", spelled "Kuf Reish Chet", but I remember that in the Passover Haggadah it's spelled differently – there it's spelled "Khof Vav Reish Khof" (which spells the Hebrew word that means "to wrap [the bitter herbs around the matzah]"). So, the members of the synagogue said, "Let's find a Haggadah and see how it is spelled there!".

They found a Haggadah and saw that the word was indeed

spelled incorrectly in the Sefer Torah. The President of the Shul ran up to the Torah reading table and said, "Put aside the Sefer Torah immediately! All these years we have been reading this verse incorrectly! You are the first one to find this mistake, so we thank you very much. But please don't show up here anymore in this synagogue. You did a great service to the synagogue for finding this mistake, but from now on, please don't come to Shul here anymore because if you are able to find a mistake in the Torah scroll, then you must not be an Am Ha'aretz, and according to our bylaws you can't be a member here any longer."

A man enters a room filled with people who are standing up one at a time and yelling out a number. Every time someone says a number, the other people in the room start laughing. The newcomer asks someone, "Why is everyone laughing whenever someone says a number?" The person responds, "They are all telling jokes. But since they don't have a lot of time, people just say a number that refers to a joke that everyone already knows." So, the newcomer decides that he will also stand up and say a number. He gets up and says, "42!". Nobody laughs. He tries another number, "87!". Still, nobody laughs. He asks the person who explained the joke number system to him, "Why doesn't anybody laugh when I say a number?" The other person tells him, "You need to know HOW to tell a joke".

Two men were riding on a train. The first man saw the second man eating something that looked like herring, so he asked him what he was eating. The other man said, "I'm eating brain food."

"Brain food? What's that?" "It's food that makes you smart if you eat it." "Really? Can I have some?" "Sure, I'll sell you some brain food for ten dollars." So, the first man bought some of the second man's herring for ten dollars and started eating it. "Wait a second!", he said. "This is just plain herring!" The first man responded, "See? You are becoming smarter already."

A young boy was in a math class in school, and the teacher posed a question for the boy: How much is two plus two? The boy thought for a minute and then said, "It depends." The teacher asked, "What does it depend on?" The boy answered, "It depends on whether you are buying or selling."

A man died and was given a choice by an angel of God to either go to Heaven or to Hell. The man said, "Before I make my decision, can I please see what Heaven is like?" The angel took the man onto an elevator which went up for a long time. Finally, the doors opened, and the man could see a very peaceful, quiet area that was sunny and pleasant. Other people were there and seemed to be happy but somewhat bored. Then the man said to the angel, "Well, Heaven seems nice enough, but can I please see what Hell looks like, just for comparison purposes?" So, the angel closed the doors on the elevator, which proceeded to go down for a long time. Eventually, the doors opened in Hell, and the man could see lots of people having a great time. They were singing and dancing, eating lots of tasty food and drinks, and there was exciting music playing in the background. Everyone seemed to be having a wonderful time. The man was very impressed with what he saw. The angel closed the doors, and the elevator went back up to the initial level.

Then the angel asked the man to make a decision. The man decided to go to Hell, since everyone there appeared to be having an amazing time and really enjoying themselves. After the angel got the man to sign the paperwork, the elevator went back down to Hell. The doors opened. This time, instead of singing and dancing, people were crying and screaming, there was fire everywhere, it was extremely hot and dry, and there was no music, no food, and no drinks. The man looked stunned and said to the angel operating the elevator, "Wait a second, the first time we were down here everyone was having a great time, and there was lots of food and music. What happened?" The angel answered him, "When you were here before, you were a tourist, so you only saw what tourists see. Now that you are a resident, you get to see what it's really like."

A factory was having a problem with a particular piece of machinery, and they called a technician. The technician said that it would cost $10,000 to fix the problem. The manager of the factory didn't want to pay that much. But the technician refused to lower his price. Finally, the manager realized that if he didn't call in the technician, then his whole factory would be at a standstill, and it would cost the company a tremendous amount of money in lost productivity. So he called the technician in to fix the broken equipment. When the technician came to the factory he spent a minute or two looking at the machine, and made a slight adjustment using one of the knobs on the machine which caused the machine to start working again. The manager was amazed, and said to the technician, "That doesn't make sense. You only spent a couple of minutes looking at the machine, and your adjustment took even less time. Why do you charge so much money to fix it?" The technician answered, "Because I know which little thing needs to be adjusted and how to do it, and you don't."

It was the day after Rosh Hashanah, which is known as the Fast of Gedaliah (in Hebrew, "Tsom Gedaliah"), which commemorates the assassination of the high ranking person named Gedaliah. A man noticed his friend eating on that day, violating the fast, and asked him why he was eating on the fast day. He answered, "There are four reasons. First, the fast should really be on Rosh Hashanah itself, but since we don't fast on a major holiday, we postpone the fast to the next day. So, today isn't the actual day of the historical event that the fast is intended to commemorate. Therefore, it is not mandatory to fast. Second, Gedaliah would have eventually died anyway, so why should I fast just because someone killed him? Third, if I had been assassinated, would Gedaliah fast for me? And fourth and finally, it is a Kal VaChomer (major to minor premise logical deduction). I don't fast on Tish'a B'Av which is a much more important fast day, so why should I fast on Tsom Gedaliah, which is a relatively minor fast day?"

My father's Talmud teacher in Winnipeg, Mr. Klein, used to tell this joke: What is Talmud? This is Talmud. There is a question: "What is it that makes a cup of tea and sugar sweet? Is it the sugar that is in the tea, or is it the stirring of the tea that makes it sweet?" The answer is: "The sugar makes it sweet". But you might say that it is the stirring that makes the tea sweet. If that is the case, then why do we need to add the sugar to the tea? You should be able to make the tea sweet just by stirring it! We must therefore conclude that the stirring is the thing that makes the tea sweet. Then why do we add sugar if the stirring makes the tea sweet? The only reason we add sugar to the tea is so that we will know when we have stirred enough (once the sugar is dissolved, you know that you can stop stirring).

A man was walking from Lithuania, where it was cold, to Southern Poland, where it was warm. He was wearing an old wool coat, and he was getting hotter and hotter. Once he got into Poland, it was too hot to wear the coat anymore. So, while crossing a bridge he threw his old coat over the side of the bridge into the river below. Another man saw that he had thrown something and asked him was he threw down to the river. He answered, "My Foo-ter" (which means "Fur Coat" in Yiddish). The word for Father in Yiddish, is Fih-ter, but in southern Poland it was pronounced "Foo-ter", which sounds just like the word for fur coat. The other man thought that the first man was referring to his own father, so he said "What! You just threw your father into the river?" The first man said "Yes, but it was an old Foo-ter (meaning an old fur coat)". The other man said, "What! Just because your father was old, that isn't a reason to throw him into the river!" The first man said, "But my Foo-ter was all worn out, and worthless, so I just wanted to get rid of it".

A joke relating to the names that are used in a Get: The rabbi asked the man who was giving his wife a Get what his name was. The man answered that his name was "Avrohom Shainis an Einikel", meaning the "grandson of Avrohom Shainis". Why was his grandfather's name Avrohom Shainis? Because it says in the Torah, Genesis 22:15, "Vayikra Malach Hashem el Avraham Shainis" (an angel of God called to Abraham a second time). The verse could also be understood to mean "an angel of God called Abraham by the name 'Shainis'".

A cantor was singing the prayer for the New Month on a Shabbat morning and came to the part where the name of the new month and the days of the week that it will fall on are announced. The Cantor sang (in Hebrew): "The month of Kislev will be on Monday, and on Tuesday, and on Wednesday". In the Jewish calendar, each month can only have either one or two days that are considered the "Rosh Chodesh" days (the beginning days of the lunar month). A congregant who was surprised by this unusual rendition of the prayer asked the Cantor, "Why did you say that the new month will occur on three days of the week instead of the usual two days?" The Cantor responded, "I needed to finish the musical phrase" (in Yiddish "Dem Tone").

Two Jewish ladies were sitting on a park bench in Miami Beach. One turned to the other and said, "You know, my synagogue just got a new rabbi, and he has a lot of sex appeal. The other lady responded, "Oh no, not another appeal!"

Humor

It was during the High Holiday services, and the Cantor sang the prayer "V'Hu Rachum" prayer which ends with the words "V'Lo Yashchis" (which means "and He won't destroy [us]"). Then, the choir responded to the Cantor with a beautiful chord and repeated the last word of the prayer "Yashchis!" (which means "He will destroy [us]!" This is funny because it is typical for the choir to repeat back to the Cantor the last word of a phrase for emphasis. But, in this case, only repeating the last word ("Yashchis" which means "He will destroy" omits the all-important word "V'Lo" which means "And He won't …".

It was approaching the time for the High Holidays, and a man was walking down a street where a few synagogues were located. The first one had a big sign on the front of the building that said, "We have the greatest Cantor in the whole city!". The second synagogue that he passed by had a bigger sign that said, "We have the greatest Cantor in the whole country!". Finally, he passed the third synagogue, and it had a little sign that said, "We have the greatest Cantor on this block!"

A man went into a restaurant for lunch and sat down to eat. After his meal, he asked the waiter for the check. The waiter told him, "There is no need for a check, just go to the cashier and pay". The man was puzzled but decided to comply. When he approached the cash register, the clerk looked at his shirt and took inventory of the various spots and splashes that were on it from the man's lunch. "Ah, I see you had the chicken soup, the pastrami sandwich and the kasha varnishkes, that'll be $12.95 please."

A teacher in Cheder (Jewish elementary school) one day was explaining the story of the Mann (known in English as the "Manna") that is described in the Torah, and how it helped to feed the Jewish people as they trekked through the wilderness after leaving Egypt, as described in the Book of Exodus. At one point in the story, the Torah text says that the Mann tasted like "Tsapichis Bidvash", the meaning of which is not entirely clear (the Hebrew word "Bidvash" clearly means "in honey", but we aren't sure exactly what the word "Tsapichis" means). One of the students raised his hand and asked the teacher, "What does that mean?" The teacher answered that it means, in Yiddish, "a Tsapichisl of D'vash" (meaning "a little Tsapichis in honey"). The student asked again, "So what is a Tsapichisl?" The teacher answered, "Let me try again to explain. The Jews were wandering in the wilderness for 40 years, and God gave them the Mann as food, and it tasted like a Tsapichisl of Dvash. Understand now?" The student asked again, "OK, but what is a Tsapichisl?" The teacher responded: "Let me try to explain it again. God took the Jews out of Egypt using great wonders and signs, and then made them wander through the wilderness for 40 years, and while they were wandering in the wilderness He gave them the Mann so that they would not be hungry, and the Mann tasted like a Tsapichisl in Dvash!". The student, who was getting frustrated at this point asked one more time, "So what exactly is the meaning of the word Tsapichisl?" The teacher responded, "Ach, I can see that you'll never understand!"

Humor

Have you ever wondered why there are so many Jewish foods with names that start with the letter "k"? For example, there are Kugel, Kreplach, Kneidlach, Kichel, Kasha, and so on. The answer is that before the destruction of the second Beit Hamikdash (Jewish Temple) these foods had similar names but without the letter "k" at the beginning of the name. After the Beit HaMikdash was destroyed, the taste of these foods was diminished due to the sadness of losing the Holy Temple. In Hebrew, the letter "k" at the beginning of a word means "like". So, originally the names were Ugel, Replach, Neidlach, Asha, and so on. But after the destruction, the names were changed to "K-Ugel", "K-Replach", "K-Neidlach", "K-ichel", "K-asha", meaning "Like Ugel", Like Replach, and so on. The foods now only taste similar to what they used to taste like, but not as tasty as before.

A woman had lent her teapot to another woman and decided that she needed it back. So, she went to the other woman and asked her to return her teapot. The other woman acted surprised, and said "I don't have your teapot". The first woman said that she remembers lending her teapot to the second woman, and now she wants it back. The second woman explained why she can't return it: "First of all, I never borrowed your teapot. Second, I already returned it. And third, it was a broken teapot anyway."

A man was going for a walk at night and noticed another man crawling around on the sidewalk, as though he was looking for something. The first man asked the second man, "What are you looking for?" He answered, "My ring. It fell off my finger down at the end of the block." The first man then asked the second man, "If you lost your ring almost a block away, then why are you looking for it here?" The other man answered, "Because there's a streetlamp here and I can see the sidewalk. Over there, it's very dark and I can't see clearly enough."

A man in ancient Greece goes into a tailor's business with torn pants. The tailor says "Uripides?" To which the man replies, "Umenedes?"

Translation: Uripides = You ripped these? Umenedes = You mend these? To fully understand this joke, you need to know that Urupides and Umenedes were famous ancient Greek playwrights, whose names sound like the phrases in the joke.

Rabbi Kravetz used to tell this riddle: What is red, hangs from the ceiling and shakes? The answer: A herring. How is that possible? First, you take a herring and paint it red. Then, you hang it from the ceiling. And finally, you shake it.

Chapter 15

Sayings and Expressions

My father had various sayings that he used to quote, and he had various expressions that he used when he spoke. Here are some of them, organized by language.

English

My father used to like quoting Professor Lieberman who said that the clever person can get out of a bad situation that the wise person knows how to avoid in the first place.

"It talks itself easier than it does itself" (probably translated from a Yiddish expression).

"If I had 88 keys and three feet, I would be a piano".

"A Truism" – My father would explain that a "truism" is a statement that is by its very definition true. It does not need to be "proved" since it is stated in such a way that it can only be true. Truisms are not very helpful in discussions since there is no point in disagreeing with them, and they don't require any real thinking.

"With that great idea, and 75 cents, I can get a ride on the subway". That was in the old days, when a ride on the subway in New York City cost less than a dollar.

"Some people won't take Yes for an answer". Meaning, sometimes people can't believe that you are actually agreeing with them, and they keep going on and on trying to convince you.

The surgeons say, "When in doubt, cut it out".

"Im-Possible" (the word impossible split into its two syllables). My father used to like quoting Sam Goldwyn as saying this (whether or not he actually said it is a matter of debate). If someone suggested something that he thought could not be done, allegedly Sam would say, "I just have two words to say about that – Im Possible."

"We are too soon old and too late smart". This is a variation of an old German saying that means essentially that by the time we attain wisdom, we are too old to make good use of it.

"The person who can't be taught anything is the one who thinks that they know everything already." An alternate version of this idea is, "People who think that they know everything already won't be able to learn anything."

If my father saw a person driving recklessly or speeding, he would say that the driver is "in a hurry to meet his Maker".

My father used to define a "Mentsch" as a person who pays their bills on time.

"Korach and His Gang" – This refers to the Biblical character Korach who had a following of people. The word in the Torah that is used to refer to Korach's followers is "Eidah" which means "congregation".

"You just had an Aha Experience" – this is an expression that the psychologists use to describe how someone feels when they suddenly understand something that previously was unclear.

"The proof of the pudding is in the eating", meaning that if you want to know whether the pudding is good you need to try it and see for yourself. My father used to mention that a lot of people say this expression incorrectly as "The proof is in the pudding", which misses the whole point of the expression.

During the High Holiday period there are four Yiddish words that start with the letter Gimmel that represent the things that we wish for most of all during the new year. The words are Glick, Gezunt, Gelt and Gedult. Glick is good luck, Gezunt is good health and Gelt is money. Finally, Gedult is patience, and it's the most important one. Because if we have enough patience, then we can eventually get all of the other things.

"Up with the good and down with the bad" – This was a phrase that my father learned at the various rehab centers that he spent time in near the end of his life. It refers to the way that a person should climb up or down stairs, one stair at a time. If you have a problem with one of your legs (the "bad" leg), when you go up the stairs you should step up using the other leg (the "good" leg). And when you go down the stairs, you should step down with the bad leg and then follow with the good leg. The theory behind this suggestion is that you can keep the leg that will receive the brunt of your body weight straight when you step down, but you need to bend your leg at the knee when you step up, which puts a lot of pressure on the knee joint. I think that he used to enjoy repeating this phrase because of its natural moral and religious connotations – you should emphasize, or "raise up", good behavior and you should avoid, or "lower", bad behavior in your life.

Latin

"De Gustibus Non Disputandum" – Literally means "Regarding taste, it is not to be disputed". This means that everyone judges for themselves whether they like something or not.

"Vita Brevis, Ars Longa" – Literally means "Life is short, art is long". This means that there isn't enough time in one's life to learn everything and to do everything.

"Post Hoc Ergo Propter Hoc – Literally means "After this therefore because of this". This is a logical fallacy that involves drawing a conclusion of causation between two events simply because one event transpired after the other event.

Hebrew and Aramaic

"Menuchosom Eiden" – This means, "Their peace should be in the Garden of Eden". My father used to use this expression when he referred to his beloved teachers who had passed away.

"Af AfAf YeOfeyf" – This Hebrew phrase means "Even the eyelash of the butterfly is flapping". It's just a silly onomatopoeic sequence of words in Hebrew that sounds funny.

"Siman Brachah" – This phrase means "A sign of blessing". My father used to quote the sentiment in the Talmud that rain is a Siman Brachah, but only if you get the right amount. Too much rain can cause a lot of damage and then is not so much a blessing.

"V'Simancha Kessef" – Literally, this means "Your sign is money". The idea is that if you want to know what the underlying reason for something is, it's usually money. In Hebrew the word Kessef means money. The Hebrew word "Siman" means a sign. In the Talmud there are various short signs, or words, which were intended as an aid to memory. The expression V'Simancha Kessef is similar to the Simancha expressions that are found in the Talmud. My father owned a book that lists many of these memory devices in the Talmud. I looked up Kessef as a Siman in that book, and I couldn't find it, which is why I believe that he meant it as an expression that sounded like the ones in the Talmud, but wasn't actually there.

"Milah B'Sela, Mishtuka Bitrain" – An Aramaic expression meaning that a word is worth a Sela, but silence is worth two Selaim (attributed to Rav Dimi in the Talmud, Megillah 18a).

"Bimdinos Eilu Uvizman Hazeh" – ("In these lands, and in our times") – My father enjoyed using this expression, which is used frequently by the Ramo (Rabbi Moshe Isserles) who wrote a commentary on the Shulchan Aruch. It means that even though in the past things were done a certain way, nowadays we do things differently due to changes in society and societal norms.

"Al Taan Ksil B'ivalto" – Literally, "Don't respond to a fool when he is ranting". There is no point in talking logically with people who are crazy or acting irrationally (Proverbs 26:4).

"Ta'an Ksil K'Ivalto" – You should respond to foolish people in the same terms that they are talking to you.

"Bat Kol" - Literally, "Daughter of a voice". This phrase appears numerous times in the Talmud, and is generally thought to mean a voice from Heaven. My father used to explain that the term simply means "an echo". So, it means a small voice, a sound that is a kind of reflection of the original voice or sound. I never heard anyone else explain that Bat Kol means an echo, but it makes sense and helps to explain the basic idea of what a Bat Kol is.

Yiddish

"Dee Ehyer Iz Lerning Dee Heener" – This means literally, "The egg is teaching the chicken." My father would say this whenever I would try to give the impression that I knew more than him on some subject, or if I would try explaining something to him that he already knew.

"The Nudnik Factor" – Sometimes, people would start questioning my father about the laws of Gittin just to be annoying, rather than trying to actually understand the law in a particular case. He would say that the "nudnik factor" was involved. The Yiddish word "nudnik" refers to someone who is annoying and bothersome for no useful purpose.

Sayings and Expressions

"Ahf-tseluches-nik" – A Yiddish word meaning someone who purposefully does the opposite of something that they should do.

"Punkt Fahrkehrt" – A Yiddish phrase meaning "The exact opposite". Some people say "Pum Fahrkehrt", but this is not the correct way to say it. The English word "punctual" comes from the same root. Someone who is an ahf-tseluches-nik will do things punkt fahrkehrt.

"Upgemixt" – A student had come into my father's class one time and seemed to be very confused about the subject being taught. My father told him "Sir, you are upgemixt". This is a Yiddish way of saying "mixed up". In Yiddish the syllable "ge" is added at the beginning of a word to indicate a past participle.

"A Glick Iz Mir GeTroffen" – Literally means "a good luck has seized me". This Yiddish expression is said sarcastically when someone tells you something that sounds good on the surface but isn't really that great, and you want them to know that.

"A Vildeh Chaya" – literally "a wild animal", which can be used to refer to a person who acts in an uncivilized way.

"Oyver Boottel" – literally means "the brain is funtioning at a diminished level", but figuratively means that something has passed its expiration date and is no good anymore. Can be used to refer to a person who is past their prime and is a "has been".

"Mirchum" (the "ch" is pronounced as in the word "cheese") – This is a shortening of the Hebrew expression "Im Yirtzeh Hashem", meaning "If God wills it". Note that the "ch" in Mirchum is pronounced as in the word "chant" or "chisel". A slightly longer shortening is "Mircheshem". Later in life, my father would use the following Hebrew expression instead of Mirchum: "B'Ezras Hashem Yisborach", meaning "With the help of the Blessed God". If I said to him, "Im Yirtzeh Hashem", he would respond "B'Ezras Hashem Yisborach". It puzzled me why he kept responding that way, instead of repeating the expression that I used. At some point, I noticed that in many of the scholarly books that he had, the phrase "B'Ezras Hashem Yisborach" appeared at the beginning of the book, and perhaps that is why he preferred to use that expression, since it is a more scholarly way of saying the same thing.

"Lo Mit an Aleph" – This expression means "No, spelled with an Aleph". In Hebrew the word "Lo" can be spelled two ways, and each way has a different meaning. If it is spelled with an Aleph as the second letter, it means "No". If it is spelled with a Vav as the second letter, it means "For him" or "To him". So, "Lo Mit an Aleph" means "Absolutely No!".

"Nisht iz Nisht" – This expression literally means "No is No". If someone doesn't want to do something, then that's fine. No need to keep trying to convince someone to do something that they don't want to do. Just move on to the next opportunity, and forget about that one.

"Tie Klippeh" (accent is on the syllable "Klip") – my father used to call his tie clip his "Tie Klipppeh", which is a play on words. The Hebrew word "Klippah" (accent is on the syllable "pah") is used in Jewish mysticism, and refers to containers which hold hidden Heavenly sparks that exist in the world and are waiting to be released. He would pronounce the word "Klippeh" in the expression "Tie Klippeh" with the accent on the first syllable to make it sound like Yiddish (and it sounds closer to the English words "Tie Clip").

"Dreying a Kop" – making one's head spin. Nudniks are very good at doing this to other people.

"Shluggin Kop in Vant" – banging one's head against a wall. This can refer to the way that one feels when trying to explain something to someone who just can't understand what you are trying to say.

"Hainu Hach Iz Dee Zelba Zach" – Litterally means "The same thing is the same thing". The Aramaic words Hainu Hach are found in the Talmud and mean "same thing", and the Yiddish words Zelba Zach means "same thing". So the whole phrase is a short poetic rhyme that explains the meaning of the Talmudic phrase "Hainu Hach".

Chapter 16

Final Years, Months, and Days

My father's final years before official retirement saw a slowdown in the number of students enrolling in his courses. For example, in the Spring semester of 1999, he taught two courses – a Talmud course on the topic of Preservation of Life, and a Codes course on Jewish Divorce. The enrollment numbers for those courses were four students and two students, respectively. One "mistake" that he apparently made was to teach mainly elective courses, which the students were easily able to avoid taking. With such dramatic declines in enrollment, it was hard to argue for postponing his retirement from JTS. If he had taught one or more required courses, which would have had much larger enrollments, then he might have had a greater chance of extending his teaching career. Word to the wise: if you are a professor, and you are reaching the end of your career, try to teach at least one required course at your institution. It might keep you employed a little bit longer, if that's what you want.

Final Years of Life

Whenever I would call my parents on the phone, I would ask my father some question about Halachah (Jewish law), or about the meaning of a verse in the Torah, or some question about the Jewish prayers. I did this so that our conversations always included some discussion of Torah in them, in order to provide my father the opportunity to earn more "extra credit" for a better life in the world to come.

Once my father turned 80 years old, I felt that there were many times in my life when I had not paid enough attention to what he was saying, and I was sure that there were many things that he said that I didn't remember. So, I made an extra effort during the next several years to listen carefully to any stories that he would tell, and to write them down so that I could remember them and preserve them. Many of those stories and thoughts are in this book.

At some point my father taught me the Yiddish word "Shlaykis", which means "suspenders" in English. I remember seeing my father's father wearing suspenders when I visited him in Winnipeg, and when he would visit us in Manhattan. The word sounded really funny, so every now and then when visiting my parents in Manhattan as they grew older, I would suddenly blurt out "Shlaykis!", and my father would laugh. It was a special way that we could share a moment of laughter together.

Final Weeks

The final weeks of my father's life were very difficult for him. He was very weak from illness. After a visit to the hospital, the doctors wanted him to stay in a rehab facility, but I thought it would be best for him to be at home to live out the final days of his life together with his wife, my mother, and I convinced the doctors to let him go home. I was glad that they agreed. I visited him as much as I could, and was able to see him very close to his passing.

Final Words

The last words that my father told me before he passed away were "Take care of yourself". This is good advice for anyone, but I especially cherish those final words, and I am glad that I had the opportunity to hear him tell me those words so close to his passing from this world to the next.

Chapter 17

List of Publications

I didn't realize how many publications my father had prepared during his lifetime until I started preparing the material for this book. I always thought that he had a hard time writing, and therefore he didn't do that much of it. And, in fact, he wrote almost no books. However, the following list that he prepared some time on or after 1993 shows that he did spend time writing, and produced a good number of articles.

Responsum in the Matter of an Agunah (in Hebrew), Conservative Judaism, 18:1 (Fall 1963).

Oxford and the Jewish Problem, Conservative Judaism, 20:1 (Fall 1965), 30-35.

Review: Boaz Cohen, Jewish and Roman Law, Tulane Law Review 41 (1966), 225-230.

The Value of Comparative Law, Conservative Judaism, 21:1 (Fall 1966), 49-56.

Hillel, Shammai and the Three Proselytes, Conservative Judaism, 21:3 (Spring 1967).

Review: Confronting Injustice: The Edmond Cahn Reader, ed. Lenore L. Cahn, American Jewish Historical Quarterly 57:2 (1967) 273f.

Questio Quid Iuris? – Some Thoughts on Jewish Law, Harvard Theological Review 61:1 (1968) 60f.

The Unfinished Task, in The Religious Dimensions of Israel – The Challenge of the Six-Day War, Synagogue Council of America, 1968, 15-25.

The Jewish Law of Divorce, National Council of Jewish Women, 1968.

On the Seventieth Anniversary of the Rabbinical Assembly, Proceedings of the Rabbinical Assembly 1970, 86-95.

Studies in Jewish Jurisprudence, Edited and with Introduction by Edward M. Gershfield, Hermon Press, New York 1971.

The Life Cycle of the Jew: A Conservative Approach. Vol IV: Divorce, United Synagogue of America, 1978.

Business Regulation and Price Control in Talmudic Economics, International Journal of Social Economics 13:9 (1986) 45-51.

May One Take the Law into One's Own Hands?, Proceedings of the Rabbinical Assembly 1986, 186-189.

Private Property in Talmudic Legal Tradition, International Journal of Social Economics 15:8 (1988) 45-53.

Review: Sidney Goldstein, Suicide in Rabbinic Literature, in Religious

Studies Review, December 1989.

The Modern Sanctity-of-Life Doctrine and the Halakhah, in Halakhah and the Modern Jew – Essays in Honor of Horace Bier, Union for Traditional Conservative Judaism 1989, 43-49.

The LBO and Jewish Law – A Rejoinder, Sh'ma 20/381 (Nov. 10, 1989).

The Homeless, a Jewish "Yes, but...", Sh'ma 22/422 (Nov. 29, 1991).

The Hebrew Language in the Legal and Theological Thought of Rabbi Moses Sofer (Schreiber), in Torah and Wisdom: Essays in Honor of Arthur Hyman, New York 1992, 49-59.

My Zaida, The Ecologist, Sh'ma 23/447 (Feb. 5, 1993).

The Problem of the Agunah – The Current Situation, United Synagogue Review, Winter 1993.

ABOUT THE AUTHOR

James N. Gershfield spent over 40 years working as a software engineer. Now, after founding Scribal Scion Publishing, he writes and publishes books on Jewish topics, as well as books that will help people improve themselves and the world.

Other books authored by James N. Gershfield:

Rainy River Girl: A Memoir (co-authored with Toby M. Gershfield)

The Illuminated Omer Counting Book (Ashkenazic Edition)

The Illuminated Omer Counting Book Sephardic Edition

www.ingramcontent.com/pod-product-compliance
Lightning Source LLC
LaVergne TN
LVHW021238080526
838199LV00088B/4568